D0331455

# THE ART OF THE
# PITCH

# THE ART OF THE PITCH

PERSUASION AND PRESENTATION
SKILLS THAT WIN BUSINESS

## PETER COUGHTER

AN ADVERTISING AGE PUBLICATION

palgrave
macmillan

Top photo on page 144 and both photos on page 145 courtesy of Avery Oldfield; bottom photo page 144 courtesy Marc Andrew Stephens.

THE ART OF THE PITCH

Copyright © Peter Coughter, 2012.

All rights reserved.

First published in 2012 by PALGRAVE MACMILLAN® in the United States—a division of St. Martin's Press LLC, 175 Fifth Avenue, New York, NY 10010.

Where this book is distributed in the UK, Europe and the rest of the world, this is by Palgrave Macmillan, a division of Macmillan Publishers Limited, registered in England, company number 785998, of Houndmills, Basingstoke, Hampshire RG21 6XS.

Palgrave Macmillan is the global academic imprint of the above companies and has companies and representatives throughout the world.

Palgrave® and Macmillan® are registered trademarks in the United States, the United Kingdom, Europe and other countries.

ISBN: 978-0-230-12051-8

Library of Congress Cataloging-in-Publication Data

Coughter, Peter.

The art of the pitch : persuasion and presentation skills that win business / by Peter Coughter.

p. cm.

"An Advertising Age Publication."

ISBN 978-0-230-12051-8 (hardcover)

1. Business presentations. 2. Persuasion (Psychology) I. Title.

HF5718.22.C68   2012

658.4'52—dc23

2011023387

A catalogue record of the book is available from the British Library.

Design by Letra Libre Inc.

First edition: January 2012

10  9  8  7  6  5  4  3  2  1

Printed in the United States of America.

*For Cynthia*

# CONTENTS

# FOREWORD

I've never met another teacher like Peter-san.

Presentation is a skill. To advance in the skill, we often resort to a formula of techniques. Because in one sense, to teach is to shape someone into a model, and that at a glance is most efficient.

But Peter-san's method is different.

What he demonstrated in our students was how to draw out their individual characteristics and let them discover their ability on their own.

Peter-san does not "teach."

"Presentation isn't only about words"—that is one of Peter-san's points. But can an American teacher educate a Japanese, in a Japanese-language presentation? Impossible? The results were amazing. The presentation skills of the Japanese participants improved dramatically.

Peter-san's method extends beyond country and language boundaries.

Finally, the most important fact of all is that what we learned from Peter-san lasts.

We easily forget what we are taught, but it's hard to forget what we discover on our own. Our students still retain in their hearts what Peter-san helped them to realize.

So the way I see it, Peter-san is not a teacher, he is a guide to discoveries. *Doshi* is a Japanese word for a person who guides another, a guru.

I think the word suits him. Thank you, Peter-Doshi.

*—Akira Kagami, executive officer and global executive creative director, Dentsu Inc.*

# THE ART OF THE
# PITCH

# INTRODUCTION

*Richmond, Virginia*

*October 1975*

John Siddall, Stanley Matus, and I started an ad agency. I was 28 years old and the youngest member of the group. We were all smart, creative, and determined to succeed. We had no idea what we didn't know. If we'd known how hard it was going to be, we never would have done it. But we didn't, so we did.

John and I were what is now known as "creatives," and Stanley was an account guy. He even owned a suit.

Most agencies get started with a "vest pocket" account, a piece of business that one of the principals brings to the new agency from his or her former employer. We had no such accounts. We did have a couple of very small pieces of business that I had been doing creative work for on a freelance basis, but they were tiny and weren't going to support three families. In fact, it was our wives who supported the three families.

We had to get some real business. But we had no idea how that was done. Cold calling companies in the Yellow Pages wasn't working. Sending letters to every company in the Red Book wasn't working. (Back in the day, the Red Book listed client companies and their agencies, with names, titles, phone numbers, mailing addresses, etc. The Internet wasn't even a gleam in anyone's eye at that moment.) And contacting people we knew, or had worked with, or maybe met in a bar, wasn't working.

But then, Reston, a new town being developed by the Gulf Oil Corporation in Fairfax County, Virginia, decided to review their advertising agency relationship. Because of John's experience on the account at his previous agency, we were given a courtesy invitation to the first round of presentations. We would be up against the incumbent, Cargill Wilson & Acree, an agency that virtually invented creative advertising in the South, which had earlier been bought by Doyle Dane Bernbach (DDB), who virtually invented creative advertising, period. Thrown into the mix were some big big-name New York agencies and the Washington, D.C., offices of yet more big big-name New York agencies. Everyone wanted this business. We needed the business.

And that's why we won the business.

It took several rounds of eliminations, multiple campaigns, countless hours of lost sleep, months of work, more than a few prayers, and a lot of presentations.

But when the dust settled, we had won. We had beaten some of the best in the business. All of who had considerably greater resources than us. All of who were, presumably, a more logical choice than three guys with no accounts, no offices, no employees, and one suit among them.

That was the moment I learned the power of presentation. The power of making an emotional connection with the audience, convincing that audience that wanting the business, and the willingness to do anything necessary to win the business, were reason enough to hire us. Simply having the best work, the best ideas, wouldn't have been enough.

Admittedly, it took a brave client, and if it weren't for their regard for John, we wouldn't have been in the room in the first place. But when the lights came on, we had to deliver. Being competitive wasn't enough. We had to be compelling. We had to convince experienced business people working for a division of one of the largest oil companies in the world that instead of one of the "brand names" in American advertising, they should hire three guys nobody had ever heard of.

And that's what we did.

In the years that followed, we fine-tuned our approach, becoming better and better at presenting. We knew that was the key to our success. In fact, it's the key to success in virtually every business. We went on to win hundreds and hundreds of creative awards, many of them on the Reston account, but we wouldn't have won any of them if we hadn't first won the business, and then learned how to sell our ideas.

The power of effective presentation was very clear to me, and I realized that even though I was the youngest and least experienced of the partners, this was where I could make a significant contribution.

We became a new business machine, winning competitions for business over agencies that were much larger and, possibly, more qualified. Not every time to be sure, but enough of the time to grow to become one of the significant agencies in the Southeast.

I learned that, regardless of the competition, if we could make what occurred in that room for two hours become the determining factor in the decision, we could beat people who should have crushed us.

Once we had the account, we worked every bit as hard to persuade our clients to produce the work that we created.

I learned how to design an effective presentation and then how to give it. Over time, we streamlined our approach to the point where I gave most of the new business presentations by myself. That's not the way it's usually done, but it worked for us.

I learned a lot in my twenty years at Siddall, Matus & Coughter. And I've never stopped learning. Today, I teach at the VCU Brandcenter, a graduate program in communications at Virginia Commonwealth University, and work with outside clients through my consulting company, Coughter & Company. Insurance executives in Illinois, creative directors in Toronto, ad folks in Japan, or students in Richmond, Virginia, all have something to teach me.

Whether it's a young creative director from Chicago attending one of our Executive Education programs who demonstrates brilliantly the power of a slide show fully in alignment with the few words he chooses to speak. Or a team of Japanese executives, who while presenting a campaign for pet food, recognizing that the judges don't speak Japanese and that they don't speak English, choose to speak "Pet," thereby hilariously persuading the audience that their approach will be most effective with pets. Or a student from my class who, with only a balloon, explains the intricacies of climate change. Or a Los Angeles-based art director tearfully thanking me because "I'm not afraid anymore."

Each of them has discovered the power within themselves. They have learned that they already know all they need to know in order to communicate effectively. They have only to unlock it from within themselves. I've just helped them find the key.

We easily forget what we are taught, but we remember what we discover on our own.

Since 1995, between teaching, training, and consulting with companies looking for ad agencies, I've witnessed 10,000 presentations. Maybe more.

I've taught somewhere around 4,000 people. When you add the 20 years I spent at Siddall, Matus & Coughter, I am well beyond Malcolm Gladwell's "10,000 Hours Rule." But as I said, I keep learning, which is the key to teaching.

I've been blessed to work with some of the smartest agencies and finest people in the field of advertising. My clients include Barbarian Group, BBDO, Boone/Oakley, Brunner, Butler Shine Stern & Partners, Campbell Ewald, Capstrat, Clear Channel Communications, Cole Weber United, Cramer-Krasselt, Crispin Porter + Bogusky, DDB, Dentsu, Draft FCB, Erwin Penland, Euro RSCG, Goodby, Silverstein & Partners, GSD&M, Hill Holliday, IPG, JWT, Leo Burnett, Modea, McKinney, Ogilvy, Publicis, Royall & Company, SandersWingo, Sid Lee, State Farm Insurance, Stone & Ward, StrawberryFrog, TAXI, The Martin Agency, Y&R, and many others.

I've also been fortunate enough to work with people in economic development, recruitment, real estate development, law, investment banking, private equity, banking, and architecture. Even basketball coaches and athletic directors on the Nike campus.

See? Everyone needs to learn how to connect. To learn how to make themselves understood. To persuade someone that their ideas are the right ideas.

I believe that all great ideas deserve a chance to live.

So let's get started.

# ONE

# EVERYTHING IS A PRESENTATION

presentation | noun

1.  The proffering or giving of something to someone, esp. as part
    of a formal ceremony: *the presentation of certificates to new
    members | the trophy presentations.*

    a.  the manner or style in which something is given, offered,
        or displayed: *the presentation of foods is designed to
        stimulate your appetite.*[1]

W hat is a presentation? We can see how the dictionary defines the word above. I like "the proffering or
giving of something to someone . . ."—like a gift.
That's a cool way to think about a presentation. And I particularly like the next part, "the manner or style in which something is
given, offered, or displayed: the presentation of foods is designed

to stimulate your appetite." That's what we want people to feel, isn't it? Stimulated. So we want to offer people a gift. Something that will stimulate their appetites for more.

We could say that our ideas are the gift, but I prefer to think of it in another way—we are the gift. We are giving ourselves to our audience. We're giving them the product of our thoughts, efforts, and personality.

We're giving them who we are. We're telling them our truth. That's our gift to them.

Most people don't think about presenting, or giving a presentation, in that way. But that's the way we should think about it—after all, we "give" a presentation, don't we?

Most people think about giving a presentation as a chore. As something difficult that they'd really rather not have to do, something to be avoided at all costs. In fact, part of why people think about presenting the wrong way is that they equate presenting with the dreaded "public speaking." I say dreaded, because in every poll ever taken of Americans' greatest fears, Number One is public speaking. Ahead of death. Every time.

But a presentation isn't "public speaking." It isn't getting up on the steps of the Forum and delivering a stentorian address. It isn't a debate. It isn't making a speech. It's a conversation. Only you're doing most of the talking. The trick is to understand that you are simply talking with your audience, sharing your thoughts. You're not arguing. You're not selling. You're having a conversation. You're giving them a gift.

## YOU'RE ALWAYS BEING JUDGED

It's *all* a presentation. I mean this. Sitting down with your boss for a little "chat" is a presentation. Going out for beers with your colleagues is a presentation. Obviously, an interview is a presentation, but so is meeting your boyfriend's family.

In each case, people are judging you. They're sizing you up. There may be a lot more on the line in one situation than there is in another, but they're still all presentations. People are forming opinions of you, opinions that are hard to change.

Often these opinions are formed when you least expect it.

For the first eleven years of its existence, the VCU Brandcenter was located downtown in a building with a fair amount of foot traffic passing by every day.

I would often stand outside and chat with a gentleman who worked upstairs from us for the Department of Transportation. He was a terrific guy and a lot of fun to talk with. One day he said to me, "This new crop of students seems a lot better than last year's." I was somewhat surprised to hear him say that, and even though it seemed he had no way of forming that opinion since he had never set foot in one of our classrooms, I asked why he thought that. "Because they don't block the sidewalk the way the kids did last year. If anyone is walking along, they get out of the way. They're courteous," he replied.

Someone is always evaluating you. Everything is a presentation.

Regardless of the situation or the stakes, I suggest that you think about presenting as an opportunity. An opportunity to share your thoughts with your audience—to give them the gift of you. Whether it's one person across a table in a cubicle or a ballroom full of automobile dealers in Las Vegas. It's an opportunity to share yourself with them.

In most business settings, presentations are team affairs. And that requires a different approach—there's a group of you, after all, and the group is going to have to come together to first agree on exactly what it is that they want the audience to take away and, secondly, how they're going to accomplish that. Each person on the team will be required to contribute to the total team argument. Each person should be "cast" for the particular skill or style that she brings to the team. And while the team has to carry the day, each individual speaker will have to pull her weight if the team is to prevail. This is accomplished principally through the process of rehearsal. We'll talk a lot more about this in a subsequent chapter, but we still shouldn't change our mindset of delivering a gift to the audience. It's just being presented by the team and not one individual. When you think about it that way, you're on the path to giving a great presentation.

## DOLLAR SIGNS

Why is it so important to be a great presenter? What's the big deal?

Why should I spend so much time and effort trying to do this when I'm good enough right now?

Because good enough isn't good enough. Because good enough will leave you in the middle of the pack. It will not get you to the head of the pack. It won't get you noticed, promoted, and compensated.

There, I said it, compensated.

There are lots of obvious reasons to want to get better at presenting, but one thing that almost no one mentions whenever I ask them why we're working on presenting, is this—money.

The first time I ever went to Crispin Porter + Bogusky, they hadn't yet opened a Boulder, Colorado, office. Everyone was still in Coconut Grove in Florida. It was a little after 9:00 A.M., and I was starting my workshop by asking the group, "Why are we working on becoming better presenters?"

Jeff Steinhour, then one of the agency partners and the head of Content Management (think Account Management), now president of the agency, was sitting in the room with 12 folks from the agency. It was my first workshop there, and he wanted to see what he had gotten his agency and his people into.

I asked the group, "Why are we doing this? Why are we spending two days trying to put on better presentations?"

I got a series of answers, all of them "right," but none of them the one I was looking for. So I went to the front of the room and I drew a giant dollar sign on my flip chart. I was a little bit afraid of appearing to be overly mercenary with an agency known for its creative commitment, but I drew it anyway.

At which point, Steinhour stood up and yelled, "Fucking A!"

Here's how it works.

If we sell the idea the first time, that work has a much better chance of being great. I don't care if you're in advertising, architecture, or investment banking. If you're dependent upon a client approving your ideas, the first one you show them is the one that has a chance to be great. It's the idea that has a chance to increase business and win awards, which, I believe, is good for everyone concerned.

But if we don't sell it the first time, if we have to go back and redo it, that costs the agency real money. Given today's tight budgets and tough compensation agreements, it's highly likely that the client won't be paying for the "redo."

Furthermore, if we sell the work the first time—the work that the agency believes is the right solution to the client's business problem—it is very likely that the work will, in fact, work, and the client will reap the rewards. More money.

---

**TAKE NOTE**

I believe that the most important job of the account leader, which is, I think, the toughest job in the agency, is to convince the client that great work is the key to success. That great work works better than good work. And that she should insist on great work from her agency.

---

And finally, if we sell the work, we become winners. We're the one the agency wants out there selling more work. To more clients. And in new business pitches. And guess what? We make more money.

It is a fact of agency life that, with very few exceptions, the highest paid people in the agency are the best presenters. Think of your shop. It's true, isn't it?

You've got to get as good as you can possibly get at presenting. Your career depends upon it. John Adams, the CEO of The Martin Agency, one of the industry's finest leaders and a fantastic presenter himself, once said to me, "I think the single most important skill anyone can have at this agency is the ability to present."

Every summer, the Brandcenter sends students who have completed their first year of study to agencies all over the world for internships. The students learn up close from some of the industry's brightest. When I ask them about their experiences, it is remarkable how many times I hear the following: "You know I worked with so and so this summer, and he's supposed to be a great creative director, but I didn't think he was really that creative." "I see," I say, "but what was he really good at?" "He was an amazing presenter," they answer.

## DO AN AD FOR YOUR ADS

Arguably the biggest complaint I hear from creatives at agencies all over the country is, "I can't get anything produced." How do you think you get to be a famous creative director? You get your work produced. And the only way you get it produced is by convincing the client that it's the right answer to their problem.

Here's a useful way to think about convincing the client that your ideas are right: Do an ad for your ads. It just doesn't matter how good the idea is unless you can persuade the person on the other side of the table to feel the same way. Whether that's your executive creative director, the client, a new business prospect, or whoever. You've got to help them get it. Whether you're a writer, art director, planner, technologist, or an account person, it doesn't matter, you're a creative person in a creative industry. You and your team have spent as much time as you could get working on your idea. Yet most agencies talk about how to present their work in the car on the way to the meeting. It's true. I've been told exactly that countless times. But there's a better way. Take some time and figure out how to sell it. Apply the same creativity and energy that went into creating the work to selling the work. Do an ad for your ads. Give your idea a chance to live. It's your baby. You've put your heart and soul into it. You can't walk into a jump ball situation and leave the outcome up to whether or not the person on the other side of the table likes your idea. I don't care if she likes your idea. I just want her to understand that it's the right idea—and that we know what it takes to achieve the goals of the brand. You've got to take control of the situation and convince her of that. So take at least a fraction of the time you spent inventing the work and create a way to sell the work. Put that creativity to work in the name of creativity. And do an ad for your ads.

## WHAT DOES AN EFFECTIVE
## PRESENTATION LOOK LIKE?

Okay, now we know why it's important to become a great presenter, but how do we do it?

Let's think about the characteristics of a great presenter and the presentations she gives.

1.  *It's a conversation, only you're doing most of the talking.*
A lot of people have a hard time with this idea. I see it almost every time I work with folks at an agency. They cling to the notion that they need to be "different" than they are in "real life," because this, after all, is work. And they want to appear "professional." What they end up accomplishing is being boring. When I sit and review presentations in one-on-one meetings with the individuals from the workshops, they are often appalled at just how boring they are. And boring is the worst thing a presenter can be. It is the mortal sin of presenting. If you are boring, you are wasting your audience's time, and they will hate you for it. Forget about being "professional," and start being yourself. Your authentic self. It shouldn't feel like an address on the steps of the Capitol or a speech at a political convention. Nor should it sound like a lecture. It should sound

the way you sound when you're sitting across the table from a friend in a restaurant.

We've all been there. Sitting in a meeting, praying for it to end while the speaker drones on about something that is apparently important to him, but of no interest to us. It might have been okay if he wasn't so stiff, so stilted, so "professional." Caught up in his own world. Lecturing us.

Don't be that guy. I can't say this strongly enough. Just talk with us. The best presenters know this, and that's how they present.

Now it goes without saying that we will turn up our volume and intensity depending on the subject and the setting. If we're talking with 5,000 auto dealers in Vegas, it's got to be a little bigger than when we're discussing the media plan with two people across a table. But it's still a conversation. Just put it into the proper proportions.

2. *Be yourself.*

Great presenters do not read their slides. I will talk about this at greater length later, but let me state it now as well, because it can't be said enough.

Great presenters remember that we're all just human. We're going to make some mistakes. There will be some slip-ups. It's okay. In fact, really good presenters acknowledge their mistakes and charm the audience by being so honest and—human.

In fact, since we're trying for a conversational style, there probably SHOULD be some mistakes. I once worked with a terrific presenter who deliberately built in a certain amount of fumbling with his words and his props—just to make himself seem like a "regular" guy. His name was Ace. His audiences loved him.

I've also worked with presenters who were too slick, too good, too polished, too sure of themselves. They came off as something less than sincere. This is also a killer. What audiences want is authenticity. They don't want a game show host.

What audiences really want, what they will really respond to is—You. I've said it earlier, but I'll say it again. Be yourself.

The best presenters know that there is no one right way to do this. There is only one Alex Bogusky, one Sally Hogshead, one Jeff Goodby. But there's also only one of you. Find your own style and exploit it. Work it. Develop it. Find YOUR voice. Don't try to sound like anyone else.

A cool way to think of it is this: You'd better be yourself—everyone else is taken.

3. *Tell stories.*

It's become a bit of a cliché, but that's probably because it's true—great presenters tell stories. We all love stories. Stories that have a beginning, a middle and an end. Stories that grab our attention right away and hold it all the way to the end. No one wants to sit through yet another boring regurgitation of everything you know about a particular subject. No one wants to watch and listen as you read from the deck. But everyone loves a story. It's arguably the oldest form of entertainment known to humankind. Since man first had language as a means of communication, we've gathered by the fire to hear the stories of the day, the tales of lives both commonplace and spectacular. Today, when we meet our friends in a restaurant, we all take turns sharing our stories and we all have a great time as a result. We need to remember this when it comes time to present to our client or new business prospect. Make it a story. Make it fun. Make it human. Make it conversational. Make it personal. Make it matter.

Get yourself and how you feel about the subject into your presentations. This is what audiences can relate to and, therefore, relate to you. That's the beginning of getting them to say yes.

So think of every presentation as a story and concentrate on creating a real attention-getting opening and a powerful close. Take them by the hand and walk them through your story to the end. That's where you get what you came for.

4. *Know Your Stuff.*

Great presenters know their stuff. They haven't memorized it. They just know it. They know it so well that they can go anywhere once the presentation starts and know exactly where they are. They can wander off on a digression if it seems like a good idea, or if they need to backtrack in order to be sure the audience understands. Nothing will solve as many problems as knowing your stuff.

Because she knows her stuff so well, the presenter is free to concentrate on the reason she's there—the audience. Great presenters are so in tune with their audience that they know exactly how they are responding. They are listening with their ears and their eyes. They're in the moment, right here, right now, totally focused, yet ready to take advantage of whatever happens in the room.

Because they know their stuff, great presenters are open to the unexpected. They just let things happen. And the unexpected is often where the fun is. People will ask crazy questions, make some bizarre statements, and, often, point out something that is actually very useful. Go with it.

Time and again in my workshops and classroom I find myself getting into stuff I never planned on discussing. And often, this is some of the best stuff said in the meeting. This can't happen if you're trying to parrot back something you memorized. And in the most practical sense, if you're counting on your memory to conjure up every single word you memorized, you are doomed. You will forget the words and then not know where you are or how to get out of it. But if you know the ideas, you'll be fine and you won't be trying to reach back into your memory and pull out the exact word you memorized. You'll simply be able to rely on knowing your stuff and delivering it to the audience.

5. *Relax and Be Personable.*

You're just talking. Don't be worried about yourself or trying to impress anybody. Because you know that the reason you're there is to get to "yes." Great presenters know that it's the audience that really counts, so all they're thinking about is the effect their words and images are having on that audience.

Be funny. But don't tell jokes.

Great presenters are humorous—they find the humor in the situations they're discussing. If you're really good at telling jokes, head to open mic night and, who knows, an HBO Special could be next.

6. *Teamwork Counts.*

In great presentations, teams present as if they really like one another. Even if you don't, find a way to at least **seem** like you do. Clients can smell it a mile away if you don't get along, and they will dismiss you immediately if they sense it.

Once I was serving as a search consultant, helping a client find the best agency for them. At one of the agencies, we got off the elevator and were met by the CEO and the chief creative officer. They seemed to be competing to see who could say hello to us first. They then couldn't decide who would lead us on the tour of the agency—the all-important Furniture Check.

We eventually got into the conference room, where we were entertained by their colleagues with a sharp, focused, creatively exciting presentation, complete with all the bells and whistles.

The two top guys seemed to demonstrate a bit of tension, but the presentation was terrific. We were handed our beautiful leave-behind books and escorted to the elevator. When we got to the bottom, I asked my clients what they thought. Wasn't that a terrific presentation? "Yes, it was very good," they said.

"But if those two guys can't get along, how are they going to work on our business?" The apparent conflict between those two individuals became more important than anything else my clients had seen in two hours. The agency was out of it, right then and there.

Great teams present seamlessly. The segues are designed to set up the next presenter.

In fact, segues add to the impact of the presentation by making it clear that this is an airtight argument that's being constructed.

### 7. *Make It Personal.*

Great presenters introduce a level of intimacy into their remarks in order to build credibility and make a connection. People respond to people. If a speaker recounts a personal anecdote, the audience often feels a kinship with the presenter because they relate the story to something that happened in their own life.

Great presenters know that, like advertising, presenting is the art of seduction, not debate. They realize that people make decisions emotionally. They will rationalize decisions based on all the facts and figures, using the objective to help them justify the decisions they made subjectively. In short, great presenters know that it's critical to make the audience FEEL that what they're suggesting is the best thing for them.

As Garr Reynolds, author of *Presentation Zen* and the blog of the same name, puts it, "you have got to be able to stand and deliver your story with clarity, conviction and grace."[2]

Your message has to be crystal clear. Your audience must understand exactly what it is that you want them to do or learn. Present with conviction. If you don't believe it, why should they? You've asked for the time to present your ideas. Let the audience see the passion that you have for those ideas. No one will care until they see how much you do.

And lastly, deliver your message with grace. Realize that it must be a show. That to really communicate effectively, you're going to have to defy conventions and do what YOU believe is right. But keep it as simple and elegant as possible.

Remember: seduction, not debate.

8. *Know Your Audience.*

The better you know your audience, the better chance you have to tell them a story that persuades them.

So know who they are as people, what they like and don't like, what they hold dear, what they believe in, what they are expecting of you and your team, and what their capacity for courage is.

I'm not saying that you must give them what they like. Not at all. I'm saying that you must know what they like in order to give them what they need.

9.  *Show No Fear.*

Everyone gets nervous. Everyone. If they say they don't, they're either lying or they're sociopaths. The trick is to use the nerves to trigger adrenaline. Let them lift you up to a higher level. A better you.

I've learned that our nervousness is never transmitted to the audience in the same proportion that we feel it. In my workshops, people will say that they were dying of nerves while presenting, but when the crowd is asked if the presenter seemed nervous, they almost always seem surprised and say "no." People who know about such things have told me that the physiological changes that occur in the human body when we're really excited and really afraid are identical. So go with really excited. Use the adrenaline.

Forget about the nerves and get on with it.

Most audiences don't know what to think. If you appear to be confident and comfortable with what you are suggesting, they are likely to feel the same way.

Remember: audiences tend to mirror the emotions we express.

*10. Rehearse.*

You've got to know your material and know it cold. Not just your part. Everyone's part. But don't memorize. Know it.

The team must rehearse together. Out loud. It is critical that everyone on the team hear everything that everyone is going to say. The team will make it better. The team will have ideas about restructuring the presentation and recrafting individual sections. But that won't happen if you don't rehearse together.

There will be no surprises on the day of the presentation, at least none caused by members of the team hearing things for the first time. That simply cannot happen.

Everyone on the team, and I mean everyone, must be present at all the rehearsals. Don't let the big boss or a senior veteran off the hook because they've done a lot of presenting over the years or they have a fancy title. If they're in the presentation, they're in the rehearsal.

You'll win a lot more if you simply rehearse.

Remember, the appearance of spontaneity is the product of preparation.

"We practiced so much, it became natural. An ironic truth," says Peter Ignazi, co-executive creative director, BBDO Toronto.

11. *Know why you're there.*

The team must agree up front on exactly what it is they are trying to achieve with their presentation. So that every step of the way, as each teammate stands to present, they are reinforcing that purpose, foreshadowing the conclusion. Nothing is included in any segment of the presentation that doesn't lead exactly to what you are there for. Keeping this in mind throughout the crafting, design, and delivery of the presentation is of paramount importance, both to the individual performances of the members of the team, and the overall impact of the presentation. I see way too many presentations in which it is obvious that the members of the team, in fact sometimes the entire team is only there to get though the deck without getting hurt. They have clearly lost sight of why they are there. Never let that happen. Knowing why you're there, and keeping it foremost in your mind while delivering your portion of the presentation, will also serve to keep you on track. Even if you momentarily lose your way, just return to the big ideas you're there to present. Since you haven't memorized the material, you won't get hung up on the words and can simply discuss the ideas.

# TWO

## IT'S NOT ABOUT YOU

The most important factor in the equation of presenting is the audience. Most people find this idea surprising, but without the audience, there is no presentation. This is a very important concept, and one that many folks fail to grasp. That deck you put together isn't a presentation. Your carefully crafted speech isn't a presentation. Nor is that pile of ads a presentation.

There is no presentation until we introduce the audience into that equation. Whether they are there in the same room with you, on the phone, or on a video hook-up, without the audience, there is no presentation. You see, you have a symbiotic relationship with the audience. Without them, there's nothing for you to do. Without you, they have no reason for being there. So you're dependent upon one another to pull this thing off.

But understandably enough, most people are so busy worrying about themselves that they don't think about it that way.

WE SHOULD PUT OURSELVES in the audience's seats and ask ourselves the following questions:

- What do you like about presentations?
- What do you hate?
- What sort of thing would you find interesting and entertaining?
- What would you find boring?

Remember, most people find most presentations boring. So don't be boring. Have some compassion for the crowd and ask yourself, would I find this interesting? Would this hold my interest?

OKAY, BACK TO THE AUDIENCE. It's always, always about the audience. Don't forget that. We're going to exercise some compassion and screen each of our ideas, indeed, everything we say and show, through the "boring prism." If you would find it boring, or if it reminds you of a presentation that you found particularly boring, take it out. If it isn't absolutely critical to your argument, take it out. If you need it to build your case, but it's boring, find a way to talk about it that isn't boring. For example, instead of discussing a demographic target for a particular product or brand with numbers, charts, and lots of type on the screen, you could substitute images of the target demographic that show them living their lives, while you describe them in your "voiceover." Maybe it needs to be explained visually. Maybe you can come up with some interesting language to explain the idea in an unexpected way. Whatever you do, you cannot be boring. Would you like to sit through another boring presentation? No? Then why should your audience have to?

## RUTHLESS EXCLUSION

In almost every presentation I see, there is at least one "WTF?" moment when I am wondering why the person is talking about a particular subject or point. It doesn't seem to be adding to the argument. It isn't going anywhere, but I can tell that the presenter finds this interesting. It isn't helping to get the team what they want; in fact, it's becoming an obstacle between them and what they want. So it must come out. We call this ruthless exclusion, and we all need to keep it in mind all the time. If it ain't helping, it's going.

We need to understand that every single thing we say must be contributing to the argument we're trying to make. Every thought we utter must be a plank in our platform, a brick in our wall. If it isn't, it must be excised. That means edited—out.

Yet I see it all the time. Everybody has good ideas at some point in time. But if it isn't the right time, it doesn't matter. Take it out.

## WHITE SPACE

*Thirty spokes share the wheel's hub,*
*It is the centre hole that makes it useful.*
*Shape clay into a vessel,*
*It is the space within that makes it useful.*
*Cut doors and windows for a room,*
*It is the holes which make it useful.*
*Therefore profit comes from what is there,*
*Usefulness from what is not there.*

—Lao Tzu, *Tao Te Ching*[1]

These words were written over 2,500 years ago. Yet they are as germane today as when the Chinese philosopher first wrote them.

This is one of the hardest lessons of all for presenters.

Artists of every kind have struggled with it for centuries.

While we're familiar with Michelangelo's claim that "It is easy. You just chip away everything that doesn't look like David," most of us don't remember this from him: "Beauty is the purgation of superfluities."

There is where elegance lies. In the removal of everything that is superfluous.

Dizzy Gillespie said, "It's taken me all my life to learn what not to play."

This is the lesson we must learn now if we are going to become great presenters. Maybe nothing else is as important.

I said earlier that my goal is for you to communicate with Clarity, Conviction, and Grace. Perhaps the most important step in accomplishing that is to understand the importance of what to leave in and what to leave out. In layout and design we call what we leave out "white space," and the term applies here perfectly.

If we were laying out an ad, we wouldn't use up all the available space with type and photos. We would leave white space to create an aesthetically pleasing message.

Then why, when it comes time to create and deliver a presentation do we cram so much information, data, type, images, ideas, and slides into it?

For some reason unknown to us, when it comes time to create and deliver a presentation, we stop being artists. We stop practicing the discipline that got us where we are in our careers. This applies to architects and urban planners as much as it does to creative directors. Everybody does it. We turn off any sense of creativity, any awareness of the craft we use in our jobs, and turn into left-brained, analytical, data-dumping automatons.

I suppose this is because we actually believe that more is more even though we all learned a long time ago that it isn't.

For the most part, we say too much. Because we haven't taken the time to figure out what's really important, but also because we think that we need to show the audience how much we know about a particular subject. We think the audience will like our presentation if it's packed with facts. It's like when we were in school back in the day and we labored under the belief that our teachers evaluated our essays by how much they weighed. Wrong on all counts. The audience does not care about how much we know. The audience cares about how interesting what we tell them about what we know is. Furthermore, the audience's ability to assimilate and retain information is limited. You're only going to be able to make two or three key points. So make them and make them memorable. You need to do this in as simple, spare, and elegant a way as possible. You're not going to bludgeon the audience into submission with a blitzkrieg of facts. It's not carpet bombing, it's a surgical strike.

You need to do everything you can to help the audience remember what they think about what you have said, because **the audience will not remember the vast majority of what you say.** But they will remember what they *thought* about what you said. And what they *felt* about what you said. So help them. Leave moments in your narrative for the audience's reflection. Be silent. Give them a chance to process and remember what they think about what you say.

It's not inappropriate to go so far as to literally say, "Think about this . . ." Or, "Imagine what it would mean if . . ." Or, "Suppose you knew that . . ." Whatever you have to say in order to get them to think for themselves about what you're saying will do the trick.

Some of the great role models for presenting are not what we would think of as "business people." They're actors. I'm not suggesting that presenting is, or should be, thought of as acting. What I am suggesting is that we have a lot to learn from observing some of the iconic film stars of our time. They know that most of acting is about listening. They know often more is communicated with silence than with words. They know that the expression on their faces says far more than words ever could. Think of Clint Eastwood. A master of minimalism.

Clint terrifies the bad guys without saying a word. Clint communicates the deepest emotions silently. Going further back, Marlon Brando, particularly in the *Godfather* films. He constructed a character of surpassing power with relatively little dialogue. He did more with an orange slice than most actors could do with a page of dialogue. Helen Mirren, in almost everything she does. Think of *The Queen*. They all exhibit great economy.

By doing this, we leave the audience the opportunity to fill in the blanks. This is where they decide what they think about what you are saying. This is what they are actually going to remember from your presentation. This is also where they find a part to play in the presentation, if you will. They are the other side of the equation, after all. This gives them a chance to play their role. It reminds me of what Howard Gossage, the legendary San Francisco ad man, said about writing ads. "When baiting a mousetrap with cheese, be sure to leave room for the mouse." Howard borrowed that line from the legendary British author and humorist who wrote under the pen name Saki.

## THE GIFT OF TIME

This notion that we have to tell the audience everything we know starts right at the beginning. You get a call from a search consultant saying you have two hours to do a credentials presentation in a week's time. What's the first thing the agency does? It calls a meeting and tries to figure out what to do for two hours, rather than figuring out what to do that will get them the business. It happens in everyday meetings with existing clients as well. We've got two hours for the meeting and we feel as if we're somehow letting them down, that we're somehow inadequate, if we don't give them two hours' worth of meeting.

That's our first mistake. The meeting should be as long as you need it to be to say what you need to say in order to get what you want. No longer and no shorter.

Use half the time and give them back an hour of their lives. They will love you for it. Time is the rarest of currencies these days and valuable beyond belief to today's overworked, stressed-out executives.

I'm not arguing for brevity for brevity's sake. Nor am I suggesting that we leave out anything that is important. On the contrary, I'm arguing that we include everything that is important and nothing that isn't.

That's the trick. Figuring that out.

Mark Twain allegedly said, "I apologize for the length of this letter, but I didn't have time to make it shorter."

There are many other quotes to this effect, but I think you get the idea. It takes time to figure out what's important. It's easy to put in everything we know. It's hard to put in only what will get us what we want.

So, start at the end and figure out exactly what it is that you want to accomplish. Whether it's just your part of the presentation or the whole thing. What do we want, and what do we have to do to get it?

Then you work your way back to the beginning.

This pertains to everything that you are going to say, but also to everything that you are going to show. We discuss the dreaded but, alas, important Deck elsewhere in this book, so suffice it to say that we need to bring the same economy to our slides. And not just the number of slides, but the number of characters on each slide. I believe the slides should be as visually powerful as possible, thereby providing context and depth for your words. Get the words off the slides. You don't need them. As I said, we've discussed this elsewhere, but remember what we said at the beginning of this chapter.

White space is good.

When I first went to teach in Japan, I was searching for a way to make this point to my non-English speaking students. I found it in a discussion of proper eating habits. *Hara hachi bu* means, roughly translated, eat until you are 80 percent full. Not 100 percent. Stop before you're full. That turned out to be a good way to explain the concept of white space. Don't fill it up, leave something empty.

You must approach your presentation practicing the lesson of *hara hachi bu*. We all fall in love with our ideas. But they're not all that interesting. We all think that it's important to let the audience see how much we know about a topic and how hard we've worked. You know what? They don't care. Take out everything that doesn't look like David.

"Make a choice about what's important and let everything else go."

—*Zen Proverb*

## LET'S GO DANCING

Most people view the idea of getting up in front of an audience with the same enthusiasm as they would approach three rounds with Mike Tyson. I suggest that we embrace the audience and acknowledge that we are in this thing together, for in fact, without the audience there is no presentation. It's just you talking to yourself.

Here's a different way to look at it: think of a presentation as a dance. You're leading the audience, but they're participating. And having fun.

It's really a kind of pas de deux, isn't it? So think of the audience as your partner, not as an adversary. Think of them as your "other half." They respond to your deft lead. You're setting the rhythm and tempo of the "music." You're in complete control, but you're exercising this control effortlessly, and they are responding to your confidence and power. And having a great time.

This shift in thinking can change everything for you. You're now constructing, choreographing and delivering this presentation with your partner, the audience, in mind. If they don't enjoy themselves, it will not have been a pleasurable experience. Make no mistake. We want them to have a good time. We want them to be entertained. If you don't think this is true, consider the alternative. This doesn't mean that the presentation has to be a laugh riot or a thrilling action adventure. But it has to be a show. It has to be time that they consider well spent. It cannot be boring. When the Dentsu executives we work with in Japan first hear this, they are surprised. Because it goes against everything they've been taught. But once they put it into practice, they blossom. The very idea that it's not just okay, but desirable, to be entertaining unlocks the door to their creativity and, sometimes, magic. And when that happens, the audience is engaged. The audience responds. The audience feels that they are a part of the show and they like that. When we do it just right, the audience and the presenter become one. Dancing together gracefully. That's when the audience really gets it. And that's the only reason we're presenting. So, if they don't get it, we've failed. Not them, us.

There are as many different ways to engage the audience as there are presentations. Here's a few examples: Start with a question. Get them talking right away. They feel like a part of the presentation and not just a passive audience. Begin by talking about them. Show their products. Pay tribute to their brand. Don't talk about yourself—talk about them. Start with an emotional story that makes the point you ultimately want to leave the audience with. Make sure it's one that the audience can relate to. Begin with a special video presenting their brand and its customers in a powerful, emotional way. Above all, be yourself. Be open and approachable. Don't try to be "professional." People have to feel that they can relate to you. That's the beginning of engagement. Here's an example from our aforementioned friends at Dentsu.

We had been working with Dentsu executives for the better part of a week. It's important to know that most of them spoke very little, if any, English, and that my colleague and I spoke even less Japanese. That's why we had four highly professional simultaneous translators in a sound booth in the back of the room. All of us were wearing headsets and microphones. We had assigned one of the Japanese teams the task of presenting a brand extension program for a pet food brand. It was critical that they demonstrate a deep understanding of the brand. With that thought in mind, a team of four stepped forward and began to speak.

"Ruff, ruff," said the first presenter. Then, "grrrrrr," growled another. Followed by "meow, meow" from the third. The fourth cooed like a bird.

They weren't speaking Japanese. And they weren't speaking English.

They were speaking "Pet."

They had briefed the translators on what they were going to do and prepared a script for them to follow along on and read as each of the presenters made the "pet sounds" and we heard them live along with the translated English in our headsets.

Needless to say, they captured the audience's attention and engagement immediately. What they said that day was very smart, but the way they said it was brilliant.

## DON'T TALK TO STRANGERS

None of us wants to fail, so how do we make sure that the audience gets us? The first step is to know who "they" are.

It's a lot easier to talk with people we know, isn't it? So try to make that happen with your presentations. In the time before your presentation, learn as much as you possibly can about the audience as a whole and as individuals. What kind of people are they? What are their demographics and cultures? Where are they on the issue you'll be talking about? What are their expectations for the meeting?

That all seems pretty logical and expected, right? But I want you to go further. I want you to find out everything you possibly can about who they are. That means finding the answers to questions like, what are their hobbies? What kinds of cars do they drive? What are their favorite movies? Do they have kids? Where did they go to school? What did they study? Are they sports fans? If so, who do they root for? And on and on. Everything you can possibly find out. Because you never know what nugget you may be able to mine that leads to a major breakthrough or helps you make a warm connection with a frosty prospect. You just never know.

---

**TAKE NOTE**

Do the same with audiences you do know. Even if it's your boss. You may think you know her, but you must always keep learning about her. You may think you know your clients well, but there is always something else to learn, not the least of which is where the votes are when you're going into a meeting. You may have thought you had the support of one person, but things have changed internally and he might just have gone over to the other side. Keep learning.

---

Don't assume that you know what your audience wants to hear. Don't assume that they know what you're there for. I've learned this the hard way. I've been on both ends of this mistake. As the presenter who assumed incorrectly what my audience was there for, and as a member of the audience wondering why the hell I was in the room listening to something that was of no interest to me or my colleagues.

So figure all this out as well. Why are they coming to the presentation and what do they expect to hear? I'm not saying that you must give them exactly what they're expecting—as a matter of fact, I suggest that you don't—but you've got to know why they're there and what they expect. After all, you can't break the rules until you know the rules.

And then, put to use what you have learned about them.

When I worked at Siddall, Matus & Coughter, we got word through the grapevine that a large account, Blue Cross/Blue Shield of the National Capital Area, was in review. They had been with J. Walter Thompson out of New York City, and had become disenchanted with the relationship. Apparently, the New York ad guys didn't want to come to Washington, preferring to have the clients fly to New York for their regular meetings. We gathered that this was the straw that broke the camel's back, so the client was looking for a new agency closer to home. I got on the phone and called the chief marketing officer, Ray Freson. Ray said that yes, they were looking closer to home, but that because of the difficulties they had had with their New York agency, they wanted to work with someone in Washington, D.C. I replied, well that's great, we're right here in Richmond, Virginia, just down the road. Ray made it clear that his bosses didn't want to go outside of the immediate D.C. area and that Richmond was just too far away. A two-hour drive was too inconvenient. I told him that the two-hour drive would be our problem. We would be happy to come to them. Ray still wasn't moved. I began to tell him about some of our clients, the vast majority of whom were headquartered in the D.C. area and advertising in D.C. media. Because Ray was paying attention to who was doing good work in the market, he knew of our work. He just didn't know that it was us who was doing it. Now that he knew of the quality of work we were doing, he said that he would try to talk the four-man committee who ran the organization into letting us into the pitch, but that he doubted they would ever actually hire someone from outside of D.C. again, let alone some guys from Richmond they'd never heard of.

True to his word, Ray went before the committee and recommended that they at least include us in the review. They agreed. We were thrilled, because I knew that if we could get the decision makers in the room, our ability to put together powerful presentations would give us at least a fighting chance. But we also realized that we had a tremendous disadvantage—we were the only contender not headquartered in the Greater Washington area. And to make matters worse, the four-man committee wanted to visit each of the contenders at their offices, and they were less than happy about having to make their way to Richmond. We said we'd come to them, but the process that Ray had designed called for agency visits, so they had to come to us.

It was at this point that I asked Ray to give me all the information he possibly could about each member of the committee. Ray, being a very savvy guy, knew exactly what I was after. Within a few days, he sent us complete dossiers on each of the four men on the committee. These documents were detailed biographies complete with photographs, so that we could call each of the men by name when they entered our conference room. We were told that we would have no access to any of them until the day of the presentation and that that one day would determine whether we advanced in the competition. It wasn't clear if there would be more than one round or not, but it was clear to us that this was our only shot. So we had better make it a good one.

I handed the dossiers over to Reid Carter, our director of research. Today, he'd be in charge of strategic planning. I asked him to read the documents carefully and try to discover something that we might be able to use to our advantage.

Reid got back to me pretty quickly, saying that there was a pattern in the dossiers that revealed something significant about common experiences and interests among all four men.

One was a graduate of West Point and had served in Vietnam. Two, one of whom had graduated from the United States Naval Academy, had served in the Marine Corps. The fourth hadn't served in the military, but listed military history as his hobby.

Now we had something. Three of these men had a strong military background and the fourth was so interested in the military that he listed military history as his hobby. About that time, a couple of us had been reading an adaptation of Sun Tzu's *The Art of War*. Originally written in the sixth century BC, this Chinese military treatise is considered the definitive work on military strategies and tactics of its time and is, in fact, still one of the essential texts. *The Art of War* is one of the oldest and most successful books on military strategy. I was reading the book because its modern translation was considered a valuable guide to strategy—not just warfare, but business strategy as well.

Since our presentation was meant to be a discussion of our credentials, we decided to present a series of case studies, each of which would be patterned on one of the key principles of Sun Tzu's book. We would present each case as if it were a military operation. We chose cases from our portfolio that lent themselves to this concept while serving to showcase dramatic success stories, or victories, in the Greater Washington, D.C., market. Of course, each of these stories also addressed a specific client need or area of concern. It's important to remember that **even when you're supposed to be talking about yourself, you should be talking about the client.**

Okay, now we've got a theme and a point of view for the presentation that seem pretty cool, but we're still the lowest of underdogs. Remember, they've already told us they won't hire an agency from outside D.C.

So we've got to do something more. We've got to grab their attention immediately and we've got to hold it until they either say yes or tell us to stop. Here's what we did. We decided that I would do the entire presentation by myself, using slides of our work, as well as a few well-chosen words, projected on a huge screen behind me.

On the morning of the presentation, the four committee members and Ray walked into our conference room, clearly unhappy to be there. We shook hands and called them by name and then, dispensing with all the pleasantries, I said, "Before we start today, I want to tell you about my favorite movie of all time." This was greeted with not just blank stares as you might expect, but actual looks of contempt. These guys didn't care about movies. But I pressed on.

"The name of that movie is *Conan the Barbarian*."

This elicited some expressions of mild interest, perhaps surprise, and just a bit of thawing in what was collectively, a very icy demeanor.

I went on. "My favorite scene in *Conan the Barbarian* is when Conan has been invited to a feast at the camp of the great general, a kind of Genghis Khan. Conan is seated on one side of the general and the general's son is seated on the opposite side. In front of them is a huge bonfire with the general's troops eating, drinking, roasting meat, singing, and telling stories. Raucous laughter fills the night. In short, a good time is being had by all.

"At one point, the general turns to his son and asks him, 'Tell me my son, what is the greatest feeling in the world?' 'That is easy, Father,' says the son. 'The greatest feeling in the world is to ride bareback on my steed across the steppes and feel the wind blowing in my hair.'

"This response does not particularly please the general, and he turns to Conan and asks him the same question. 'Conan, what is the greatest feeling in the world?' Conan looks him in the eye and says, 'The greatest feeling in the world is to crush your enemies, to see them driven before you, and to hear the lamentations of their women.'"

I waited a beat while the audience looked at me in astonishment. And then I said, "And that's what we think advertising is about.

"And that's why today's presentation is called 'The Art of War.'"

At which point the title slide appeared behind me in red type on a black background.

At this point, the audience was beaming. One of the men actually clapped. They hadn't ever seen anything like this. It wasn't something they were expecting, but they liked it.

I immediately got into the show and kept it moving. They were nodding and smiling throughout. At one point, the gentleman who had listed military history as his hobby was reciting the St. Crispin's Day speech from *Henry V*. That is one moment I will never forget.

I will also never forget that they promised us the account then and there. They said they still had to see another agency, but they liked what we had shown them so much that they felt comfortable promising us their business.

They were as good as their word.

We went to work shortly thereafter and did excellent work for over five years. Ray Freson turned out to be a terrific partner, and we enjoyed a wonderful relationship with virtually everyone involved in the marketing program, producing results far in excess of their projections.

It all happened because we thought to ask, "Please tell us everything you can about these people."

Here's a story that illustrates the point in another way. It's from Bill Westbrook, a former colleague, and former vice chairman of Fallon.

Before Bill went to Fallon, he was creating great work and leading new business teams at The Martin Agency and Earle Palmer Brown.

*The single best presentation moment I ever witnessed came in the mid-1990s when Scali McCabe Sloves and The Martin Agency combined to pitch for the Mercedes business.*

*A little background: Lexus was touted as "The New Definition of Luxury" and was seriously kicking Mercedes' ass. Plus Mercedes hadn't introduced new metal in a few years and was seen as tired, old-school luxury, and boring. The Germans were understandably concerned, even anguished, and called for an agency review.*

*On the other side, Scali was a shadow of its former self. McCabe had long since gone off. The agency had shrunk dramatically, although it still had pride. And to top it off, it had lost Volvo recently after being accused of rigging a television spot focusing on safety, Volvo's core equity.*

*I was asked to run the pitch on behalf of the combined agencies, which ran for several months and many, many meetings and mini-presentations. Martin wanted to win, but Scali simply had to win to even continue as an agency.*

*Presentation day arrived. I had decided that Marvin Sloves, as the head of the lead agency, should start us off and "set the table." The Germans marched in wearing their Hugo Boss suits, very dignified and somber. The agency team sat at another table, nervous and tight.*

*As Marvin was preparing to rise, I touched his arm to wait a moment. Leaning in to whisper, I said, "Marvin, this is for everything you've worked your whole life to create. It comes down to this moment. You have to go out there and kill it, make them love us right now, and inspire the team, even frighten the team that we can never live up to what you're about to do. Do it, Marvin. This is your chance for redemption."*

*Marvin breathed deeply and raised his head theatrically and rose to walk to the center of the room to begin.*

*He said, "100 years ago there was a clown, a German metaphysical clown named Valentine. And as part of his act he would walk out onto a darkened stage illuminated by a single beam of light in the corner. He would walk over to that spot and fall to his knees and begin frantically looking for something on the stage."*

*At this point, everyone on the Scali/Martin team had their mouths open in fear. Where was this going? But as I looked at the Germans . . . they were nodding! They knew the story! It was true!*

*"As part of the act, a policeman walked out onto the stage and asked what Valentine was doing. 'Oh, I've lost my keys,' the clown replied, and immediately the policeman fell to his knees to help. After a few moments, the exasperated policeman rose, dusted off his pants, and asked 'Are you sure you lost your keys here?' Valentine said, 'No, I lost them over there,' and pointed to the darkest part of the stage. 'Then why are you looking for your keys here?' asked the frustrated policeman.*

*"Valentine answered, 'Because this is where the light is.'"*

*Then Marvin approached the Mercedes team and said, "Now is a hard time for Mercedes. It feels like you have lost your way. But all that's happened is that you've temporarily lost your keys and you've been looking in the wrong places for them. In the next two hours, we're going to help you find them again.*

*"Bill . . ."*

*I had to stand up in the midst of full-throated cheers and applause and follow that story.*

**—Bill Westbrook, former chief executive officer, Fallon**

Apparently, he and his teammates followed it well, as the combined Scali McCabe Sloves/The Martin Agency team won the account. The win brought Scali back to life and moved The Martin Agency up another level in prominence.

Don't ever talk to strangers.

Those stories illustrate perfectly the importance of knowing your audience and understanding how to reach them. Here's a story from Jim Othmer that demonstrates what can happen when you not only don't know enough about the audience, you manage to *confuse them with another client.*

*During a major dog and pony show, in front of more than 100 franchisees gathered at the client's global headquarters, my executive creative director set up my presentation by telling a long, passionate tale about her (and the world's!) affection for the legendary figure that was synonymous with their brand. "Everyone loves The Captain," she began. "The Captain is one of the most beloved characters in all of advertising, and at all costs, it is our responsibility—no, mission!—to keep the brand mythology of the Captain alive." At this point the franchisees were mumbling and shaking their heads and I had broken into a sweat. Before taking the floor to present work that was certain to die a deep-fried death, I looked the lead account person in the eye and said, "Holy Shit. She confused Crunch with Sanders." Not only had she gotten the Colonel's title wrong, she had busted him in rank. Our work and our affinity for the brand suddenly seemed half as genuine.*

—**James P. Othmer, author of** *The Futurist* **and** *Adland*

# THREE

# HOW WE CONNECT

All right, we're dancing with the audience and we're not dancing with a stranger. We know everything we possibly can about them.

Presumably, they know a lot about us as well. But how do we make the connection that will get us what we want?

First, we need to understand how the audience decides about us and what we have to say. Well, they listen to us and they make up their minds, right? No, not exactly. And as we said earlier, I don't believe they remember a lot about what we actually say. They look at us and listen to us and begin to form an opinion.

There has been a good deal of research done on exactly how people take information away from a presentation. The findings in all the studies are remarkably similar. You may find what they reveal to be surprising.

The best known and most referenced study was done by Professor Albert Mehrabian of UCLA in the 1960s.[1] What Dr. Mehrabian posited was that there are three categories of stimulus present in human communication—the Visual, the Tone of Voice, and the Words used (spoken or read). He suggested that 55 percent of what we take away from communication comes from the visual, 38 percent from the tone of voice, and 7 percent from the actual words.

While the numbers he suggested might not be precisely the same for all presentations in all settings, I do believe, based on everything I've seen and learned over the years, that thinking about presentations in this way will lead to simpler, more elegant, and more effective communication.

And his work supports my contention that people won't remember most of what we say—but they will remember what *they* think and feel about what we say.

It's clear that the research is a confirmation of what many of us have suspected/feared/known for a long time: the way we say something is more important than what we say. The tone we use establishes our attitude, and our audience takes its cues from that attitude. Our audience decides an awful lot of what they think about us and what we're saying based upon that attitude. Notice I said that they decide an awful lot of what they think about *us,* and what we're saying based upon our attitude. What they think about *us* is absolutely critical. As we've seen, it's more important than what we say. They're deciding, "Do I like this person? Do I trust her? Do I want to do business with her? Would I like to go have a beer with this guy at the end of the day? Do I think he knows what he's talking about?"

They're deciding all that and more, based upon your attitude. If we sound and seem confident, they will tend to believe us and share that sense of confidence. If we are enthusiastic, they will tend to be excited about what we're saying. In short, the audience will tend to mirror the emotion that we establish via our attitude.

If you don't think that's true, here's a story. One art director/writer team at the Brandcenter presented their concepts to a group of Brandcenter board members. They showed very little emotion or excitement for their work and essentially slid it across the table, figuratively saying, "Here it is, how do you like it?" The board members were united in their ambivalence. They didn't think much of it at all. They were trying to be nice to the students, but it was clear that they really didn't like the work.

---

### TAKE NOTE

I believe most audiences don't know what they like or dislike and have to be "told" what to think. They are "told" by the way in which we show them things whether they should like it or not. I really believe this and I really believe it is an incredibly important thing to remember.

---

The same team then took the exact same work down the hall to another group of Brandcenter board members. I tagged along and told them to really *present* the work this time. To use some of the skills they had learned in school. They presented the work with enthusiasm. They presented with clarity, conviction, and grace. The board members loved the campaign—the exact same campaign that had left the previous group cold.

I huddled with the student team afterwards, and they said, "You know, we thought you were right, but we just wanted to see for ourselves. That was exactly the same campaign, but it got two completely different reactions. It was all because in the second group we *actually presented* the work. From now on, that's what we're gonna do." I hope they do.

But if you don't believe me, let's listen to Dr. Joel Whalen in his 1996 book, *I See What You Mean*: "Your attitude is the power that drives the most important and powerful symbols you communicate. To be a great oral communicator, you must first manage your attitude. It's the way you say your words that makes you persuasive. In fact, the words you use in oral communication are only minor parts of the message your listeners receive."[2]

## WHAT THEY SEE IS WHAT YOU'LL GET

Before you've even said a word, your audience is sizing you up. They're looking at your wardrobe, your jewelry, your haircut, your posture, and all the other nonverbal signals you're sending. Based on this, they make a judgment about you and decide right then and there whether they find you credible or not. You haven't even said a word. Is this fair? I really don't know, because it doesn't matter if it's fair, it just is.

Your visual aids are also a powerful communicator. Be they slides, charts, boards, props, videos, or a combination of all the above and more, they should be chosen carefully. Above all, they should be simple. Simplify, simplify, simplify. It's what we should be doing as advertising people, yet we often forget that when we're crafting a presentation. As we said a bit earlier, one of the most common mistakes in presentations is the inclination to put in everything we know about a given subject. This will not work unless your objective is to confuse your audience. We must use as much discretion as possible to eliminate all facts that are not critical. And the definition of critical for me is whether they are necessary to get what I want. If not, we must take them out, no matter how fascinating they may be. Ruthless exclusion, remember?

The visual presentation is critically important to the overall pitch—but remember: make the deck as simple as possible. Use visuals, not words. If you must use words, limit them as much as possible. And do not read them. Never read the words on your slides. Are there exceptions to this? Of course, as with all rules, there are exceptions. But I can't say this strongly enough about this. **Do not read the slides.** Your audience can read perfectly well, thank you.

Also, it's important to remember that the visuals aren't simply what's on the screen, or on boards, or props that you may use. *You* are a part of the visual look of the presentation. This goes for every person and everything that the audience sees.

When used properly, visuals can lend a rich emotional context to the words you're saying, resulting in powerful, memorable communication.

Think about your presentation the same way an artist thinks about creating a music video, or a motion picture. The images tell much of the story. The images can convey meaning beyond the capacity of words. We all know this, but we forget it when putting together a presentation. If you're going to use slides, let them work for you.

One of the iconic images in the history of motion pictures, and one that has been copied incessantly, is a scene from the motion picture *Patton,* starring George C. Scott.

The screen is filled with the image of an American flag stretching the length and breadth of the frame. In front of this flag, General Patton strides onto the stage and delivers his message to the audience. That image of George C. Scott in front of the American flag speaks volumes and is the single most memorable moment in the film.

The image of the flag perfectly complements the lines that Francis Ford Coppola wrote for Scott to deliver. The images and attitude work perfectly to deliver the message.

So think about what your slides say. Would they say more if they were more visual? Would they actually "say" more if there were no words on the slides?

We all know the ancient adage that "a picture is worth a thousand words." Yet we seem to forget it when we're putting together our presentations. That's because we're lazy and often just project the deck onto the screen. We'll deal with that in depth in chapter 12, but let's concentrate a bit more on visuals for a moment. If you're talking about a target audience, why not *show* me the target audience rather than use type that *says* "Adults 18–34"? Show me some adults 18–34. If you're talking about what people want or expect from a product, show me what they want and expect. If we're talking about kids, show me some kids. Your audience will respond emotionally to images and the words you say to accompany those images. They will not respond emotionally to type on a screen. If you want to win, if you want to get what you want, you must make your audience respond emotionally. One powerful way to achieve this emotional connection is through visuals. And while we're on the subject, work very hard to be sure that your visuals are in alignment with what you're saying. Your visuals should be in harmony with your words. They should appear on the screen at exactly the right moment. Not before and not after. That's one reason I often suggest the use of a black slide at the beginning of a presentation and then whenever it's appropriate during a presentation. Let's not have anything on the screen that doesn't purposefully support the point we're trying to make.

Let's talk about the visual impression of your presentation in another important way. Since 55 percent of what people take away from a presentation is visual, it stands to reason that 55 percent of what people believe about a presentation and the presenter is visual. If you appear to believe in what you're saying, they will believe in it.

If you are slumping and staring at the floor while claiming to be excited, they will not think that you are excited. They will not believe you. Worse, they will think you're lying. Not good.

Lastly, what about the words we use? People often ask me, "Do you mean to say that the content of my presentation is only 7 percent of what people take away?"

No, I don't. What you need to understand is that everything—your tone of voice, the way you look, dress, move, your slides, and your words—is the content. All of it. It all works together if we're doing it right. Some parts of it are more important than others, but it's all of a piece.

And even if the words we say are of very low priority in the decision-making hierarchy, I suggest that we choose them very carefully. Use vivid, colorful language. Use powerful words that create an image in the audience's mind.

People tend to like what they picture in their own minds. They're seeing it their way. So they like it. That's why I've become convinced that the best way to present a television commercial is to tell the story of the commercial rather than taking the audience through a storyboard or using a key frame. (It also avoids the inevitable "but on the storyboard she was wearing a blue blouse" comment while you're on the shoot.)

I asked you earlier to make your audience remember what they thought about what you said. This is consistent with telling them the story of the commercial and letting them picture it their heads.

Avoid clichés. Use interesting, powerful language that makes you seem thoughtful. I don't mean "considerate," I mean full of ideas.

"I have a dream."

"Yes we can."

"I feel your pain."

"You have a branding problem masquerading as an advertising issue."

"When I was 24, I met a Spanish chef."

"If the British Empire and its Commonwealth last for a thousand years, men will still say, 'This was their finest hour.'"

"Ask not what your country can do for you, ask what you can do for your country."

So remember the power of tone and attitude and incorporate that understanding into your presentation. Above all, remember the power of visuals, because what your audience sees will play a major role in what you get.

I consider the research on how people take away information from a presentation to be directional more than literal. I think the way people perceive a presentation varies from day to day and show to show. Nonetheless, the importance of connecting remains paramount.

## WHY IT'S CRITICAL TO CONNECT

There's a real temptation to take it for granted that we must connect, but I've seen too many presentations in which it was clear that the presenter(s) didn't really place any priority on connecting. They were there to do "their part" and return safely to their own private world.

The advertising industry evaluates careers and agencies based on the work that gets *produced*. Buildings the size of Madison Square Garden are filled with stacks of great work that didn't get produced. Great ads that the client "didn't get." Brilliant television concepts that "are smarter than my creative director." Digital concepts that are "beyond the CMO's taste level."

For every ten "great" pieces of advertising that get created, maybe one is produced. And for some agencies, I'm being generous. Why do you think that is? To continue in the spirit of generosity, it's possible that there is the occasional case of "pearls before swine," but more often than not, it's the creator's ability (or that of her surrogate) to *successfully connect* with the audience that carries the day. Whether it's internally with the creative director, or the account team, or even an agency principal. Or, more often, with the client. If we don't connect, we don't sell the work, and if we don't sell the work, it doesn't get produced, so no one will ever know how brilliant our work is and the client will not have the benefit of that work helping her company.

And don't even begin to talk about the work that gets presented in new business competitions. In the vast majority of cases, the work presented by the *winning* agency never gets produced. There are a lot of reasons for this last instance, not the least of which is that the work is often produced in a vacuum, without any input from the client along the way—but in some ways, this is just an excuse.

In the last chapter we featured a story from Bill Westbrook, who has been vice chairman, president, and chief creative officer of some of the best advertising agencies in the world. He has won every creative award worth winning. But if someone were to ask any of the thousands of people who know him to identify his most significant asset, the thing that he probably does best and is best known for, they would cite his talent as a presenter. Isn't it surprising that such an accomplished creative advertising person is first recognized as a presenter? Actually, it isn't surprising at all. Over the years, I've learned that there is a very high correlation between creative reputation and ability to present. This is not to imply in any way that Bill's reputation is based primarily on his ability to talk about creative, because he is legitimately a creative powerhouse. I would rather explain the correlation between Bill's creative reputation and his reputation as a presenter much the way he would.

Because I can tell you that the vast majority of the work Bill presented in new business competitions actually got produced.

Why is his record any better than that of most agencies? One simple reason: he is one of the best presenters who ever walked into a room. He makes a connection with his audience. He and his agency developed a reputation for brilliant creative work because the work that they believed in, their best work, got produced. And it got produced because of his ability to sell the work. For many people in advertising, "sell" is a dirty word.

**TAKE NOTE**

Our friend Alex Bogusky, one of the most successful creative people of our time, argues that he doesn't sell the work, rather that he has a "conversation" with the client, and together they decide that the work is right. I completely agree that the process should be a conversation, but the product of that conversation is the successful sale of our ideas. And Alex is an amazing presenter.

This aversion to selling has always struck me as odd, given the fact that most of what advertising people do is create work that is designed to sell things or ideas. We get paid to move product. Whether it's TV sets, sneakers, cell phones, or even "good causes." But there is still some kind of Willy Loman–like image conjured up in the minds of creative types when one utters the word "sell." This is a particular problem for a lot of young people either in, or aspiring to be in, the business. I see these folks all the time. They think it's somehow uncool to have to sell their work. Until they overcome that problem, they will continue to have their most beloved ideas rejected while they and their agencies end up producing work that doesn't please anyone (including the intended audience.) Yet many young people shrink from the idea of "selling" their work. They need to learn the lesson of Bill Westbrook. They need to learn that it is cool to be a good presenter.

Speaking of good presenters, Jeff Steinhour, president of Crispin Porter + Bogusky, is a great presenter. He is often called upon to advise advertising students and he never fails to emphasize the importance of presenting Here's some important advice from Jeff for young people who are still in school: "Volunteer to present something in front of a group every day from now until you graduate. For real. There's one immutable truth to the advertising business: best presenter usually wins. You can't avoid it. It's like a fireman being afraid to go to a fire. Can't happen. Face it now and get good at it. Then get great at it."

What makes anyone a great presenter? More than anything—he has the courage to be himself. We talk about this idea elsewhere in this book, but I'll say it here as well—there is no one right way to present. There are certain fundamentals that need to be considered in any presentation, but there is no one right way to be. When I say "to be," I'm referring to the personality or persona that we present to our audience. Just be yourself. Don't try to be someone else. Being someone else doesn't work. This isn't acting, this is business. So it comes down to confidence. The confidence to be who you are. There is really nothing so powerful as the force of an individual's personality passionately displayed.

This idea is completely foreign to many people. They assume that if they are to give a "presentation," well, they'll have to turn into the kind of person who gives a "presentation." They then proceed to try to do an impression of whomever they see in their minds as the kind of person who gives "presentations."

This results in taking the audience further and further away from any authentic representation of oneself, and ultimately, to the same boring, catatonia-inducing presentations that we've come to expect.

You see, many of us have an idea of what the ideal presentation is—and it's completely wrong. We've been taught by experience that presenters are very "businesslike" or "professional," words that are actually code for boring or robotic. We expect presentations to be a certain way based upon what we've learned, which, unfortunately, is usually wrong.

As we've said, presentations should be just like a conversation. Only you're doing most of the talking. They should feel as comfortable as a conversation with a friend. I say "a" friend because we want to create the feeling in the room (or on the phone) that we're talking to just one person. So no matter how many people are viewing the presentation, we approach it as if we were talking to one person. A good way to think about it is as if you were in a restaurant with a close friend chatting with her about what you did that day.

You wouldn't be playing a role. You'd be yourself. If you weren't, your friend would wonder what you were doing. Has she lost her mind? That's exactly what goes on in a presentation when we try to be someone we're not. We're not good at it. Most of us are not good actors. If we are, we're probably in the wrong business.

What we are good at is being ourselves. Being our authentic, down-to-earth selves. That is the only platform from which we can speak sincerely. That's the only way we're ever going to be able to build genuine trust. And without trust, we will never accomplish anything of significance in our business relationships.

Being who we are is interesting. As Roger Ailes said many years ago, you are the message.

There is only one you. You are unique in the true definition of the word.

The audience isn't there to read the screen or look at your boards or other visual props, they are there to hear from you.

So let them. Give them you.

Being who we are is powerful.

Being our true selves accelerates and enhances human connection.

And as humans, we connect emotionally—soul to soul, not mouth to ear.

Here's an example of what I mean:

*In 1992, one of the partners left our agency and everyone in the press was speculating that we'd lose all our magic in new business situations. This of course made us ripe for a vast over-compensation when it came to our next pitch. Sure enough, we got a call from Doug Glen at Sega, who told us they had a brief window in which their 16-bit Sega Genesis would be obviously superior to the 8-bit Nintendo system, so everything had to happen quickly. Not only that, but we'd be up against what was probably our fiercest competitor, Wieden + Kennedy in Portland.*

*This is a story of swarming and complete involvement.*

*The swarming came in the form of proving out every possible competitive advantage we had. We asked tons of questions and appeared at their offices regularly, just to show how much closer we were, here in San Francisco, than the Oregon agency. We prepared a video that showed people up on our roof, hitting the Sega building (25 miles down the road) with golf balls (we actually bounced the balls off their windows), and proclaimed, "We're just a short drive away." We talked to their suppliers, their programmers, even venture capitalists who competed against them.*

*We hired 12-year-old business consultants and ran all our ideas by them. And in the end, we even shot cheap mock-up commercials, in a day when people didn't do that.*

*Sega told us that the pitch had to take place in a Holiday Inn in Mountain View, California. We looked at the room—a typical convention meeting room, with folding chairs. So we transformed it.*

*First, we brought in bleachers and surrounded the room with them. We rented a sound system that the Grateful Dead used when they played local clubs. When people entered the room on the day, they encountered a young boy sitting cross-*

*legged, playing the most recent Sega games on a stack of wide-screen TVs, engineered to become one big, three-by-three screen game system. The sound was thunderous.*

*When everyone was seated, I had the privilege of pointing to the throng of people up in the stands around them. "These are the people of our company, all of them," I said. "You're probably wondering why they're here. Well, as a matter of fact, every one of them is now an expert in Sega. Because for the past month, each of them was assigned the job of knowing one of your games intimately. Every single game you've ever published is represented in these stands. If you ask for a 'Sonic II' expert, there is one up there. If you ask for a 'Battletoads' expert, there's one of those. 'Ariel the Little Mermaid.' 'Monopoly.' They're all out there. Ask a question. Go ahead."*

*We passed out amazing blue and white letterman jackets that commemorated the fact that you'd been at our pitch that day. (I still have mine.) We gave them tapes to take home. One of our account guys, in a Sonic the Hedgehog suit, hugged them all before they left.*

*When the meeting was over, we dismantled the set and made it back into a fuchsia meeting room. Then, we went home. It was like we'd never been there.*

*They gave us the business the next day.*

—Jeff Goodby, co-chairman
and creative director,
Goodby, Silverstein and Partners

# FOUR

# THE POWER OF EMOTION

True human connection is a bond that is based upon emotion. In order to create this, we must be honest, open, and sincere. We must show what we truly feel, not just what we believe. Human connections are emotional. The power of emotion is what bonds us together and builds trust.

Without trust, we will never achieve what we want.

Most people I know would never think of lying in a meeting or an interview, yet when they try to be someone they're not, they're lying, aren't they?

The very best way to convey emotion is by being ourselves— by showing the audience how we *feel* about what we're talking about. We can only do this if we're telling the truth—*our* truth. Getting this thought through our heads, truly believing it, is a major breakthrough for many of us. We find it powerfully liberating, as well we should, because we no longer feel the strain of trying to be someone we're not, or of trying to behave in a way that is foreign to us.

Who you *really* are is far more interesting than who you *think* they want to believe you are.

One of the most gratifying feelings I've ever gotten from my workshops—and I'm pleased to say, I've gotten it many times—is from people who come up to me at the end, or email me days later, or tell me the next time I'm back at their agency, "It's so great to realize that I can just be me."

There is a wonderful creative director at Wieden + Kennedy Brazil named Guillermo Vega. Guille is from Argentina, and English is a second language for him. He is embarrassed by his command of English, but he shouldn't be because he is a marvelous presenter. How can this be? Because Guille is Guille. He doesn't attempt to be anyone else. He is funny, smart, and passionate. His love for his work comes shining through. His enthusiasm is infectious. It is impossible not to like Guille. And so, we like his work. There is only one Guille. If anyone else attempted to present like him, it would be a colossal failure. Yet Guille is effective precisely because he is who he is.

The aforementioned Bill Westbrook is a great example of the same phenomenon. He is who he is and that's plenty good enough. Bill is from the "high risk–high gain" school of presenting. By this I mean that he's not afraid to take chances. To reach for the powerful moment that others might resist. Some might call him flamboyant, almost theatrical in his persona, but it never appears to be contrived. Because it isn't. He reaches down inside himself and finds the absolute truth of the situation—his truth—what he believes deeply about the subject—and presents it in a powerful, compelling way.

Once, at a major new business presentation, standing in front of a long table of client representatives, he began to speak to just one woman, seemingly ignoring the rest. He spoke to her very quietly, as if she was the only person in the room. Amazingly, he wasn't speaking about advertising at all. He was talking with the woman about her personal fears and desires. About her hopes and regrets. About how she felt about her body, her self-image. And slowly, but surely, he began to reach her. And soon, he began to reach the rest of the client panel who were mesmerized by this singular focus on just one person. After a few minutes more, the woman he was speaking to began to cry softly. Not because she felt afraid, or abused, but because she had been so deeply touched by what Bill had said. At that moment, he turned to the huge screen behind him and unveiled the central theme of the presentation. The entire panel of judges was eventually carried away on the same tide of emotion that had first gathered up that one woman. And so, Earle Palmer Brown won the Weight Watchers account.

That's why I referred to his style as "high risk–high gain." Very few of us would have the courage to attempt such a strategy.

Even fewer could pull it off. But Bill knew that the key to winning, the key to persuading the panel, was to reach them emotionally. He had to find a way to immediately place the group in an emotional context. He changed the rules. He broke with convention. He shifted the dialogue to the emotional side of the panel's collective brain and away from the analytical. He took the chance of talking with a woman about her personal struggles with her weight. And it paid off. Mind you, he had brilliant creative work born of sound strategic insights to back him up. But at the level he was playing, all the agencies had that. He brought emotion to the table.

Once, my agency was presenting in the finals for the State of Virginia Department of Tourism account. By law, the agency-client relationship had to be reviewed every four years, and the competition was always intense. The Martin Agency had created the well-known "Virginia is for Lovers" campaign back in 1969 and, unlike many other states, the Virginia Department of Tourism appreciated good creative work. So every agency wanted the account.

I wasn't born in Virginia, but I've spent the majority of my life there. I got my first real job in Virginia. I met the woman who became my wife in Virginia. Our two boys were born there. I started a company with two partners that grew and prospered there. I cared about it very much then, and I still do. So I made sure to say that in my presentation. I made sure that the judges understood my feelings for the Commonwealth. I did the entire one-and-a-half-hour presentation by myself, but I made it clear that our whole agency felt the same way. I didn't talk very much about what I thought about Virginia as a travel destination, but rather, I talked about what I *felt* about Virginia as a travel destination. And I talked a great deal about the way visitors would *feel* when they came to Virginia. We put together a presentation that was simple, visually arresting, and overwhelmingly emotional. I delivered a closing statement about how much I felt I owed to the State of Virginia, my gratitude to the state for making so many of the significant moments in my life possible, and my love for the place. I walked off the stage as a three and a half minute video featuring beautiful images of the Commonwealth accompanied by a wonderful piece of original music written by our friends Robbin Thompson and Carlos Chafin began to play. As the video played, I looked out into the darkened room at the panel of judges. You could see the emotion on every one of their faces. I knew we had won. And we had. They hired us because of the way we felt about the Commonwealth of Virginia. They hired us because we were able to put into words the feelings that they, too, had for the state. Not because of what we said we would do, but because of how we made them feel.

What these two stories have in common is the fact that in both Earle Palmer Brown's case and ours, we found a way to touch our audience emotionally. We both set an emotional tone from the very beginning. Most agencies never do. They attack the other side of the brain. This is a common mistake. The essence of selling is emotion. Virtually nothing is sold on the rational, analytical level. Oh sure, we tell ourselves that we got a great deal on that new car in the driveway, and that it's one of the safest cars on the road, with a record of great resale value, and it gets surprisingly good mileage. But the real reason we bought the car is that we like it. It makes us feel good. We feel good sitting in it. We feel we deserve it. And it delivers a message about us that we want the neighbors (if not the world) to hear. It's all about feeling. How we feel, and how we believe others will feel about us.

So we've got to make our audience feel something. That doesn't mean we've got to make them cry. Maybe we need to make them laugh. Maybe we need to make them remember the way they felt when they were in a particular situation that's relevant to the subject at hand. Maybe we need to make them feel that we really know what we're talking about. Or that they would really like to spend more time with the people on our team. Or that their careers would be enhanced by working with us. I could go on and on, but you get the point. Facts may impress them, but feelings will persuade them. We've got to make emotional contact. But how do we do that?

We start by remembering that we're all human. And as human beings, we're emotional creatures. Regardless of our age, race, background, education, or any of a hundred other qualifiers, there is a common human experience that we all share. It's our job to tap into the "collective unconscious" and extract the artifact that strikes the right chord with our audience. Whether it's a woman's struggles with her own self-image or the feelings we all share for the place we call home. It can be the telling of a story, a piece of music, or an image on a screen. It can be any of a thousand different things. There are examples of this all around us everyday. Why are certain books popular, and others not? Why does an obscure news story from a small town in Oklahoma capture the imagination of the country? Why does a particular movie seem to touch all the right buttons? Because of the skillful application of emotion.

## THE SECRET TO SELLING
## CREATIVE: FRAMING

Most agencies and many creative people have a common complaint—they can't sell their best work. There are many different reasons for this, among them the naïve notion that great work will sell itself or that, ultimately, great work will rise to the top. Anyone who's been in the business for any length of time knows how false these assumptions are. Great work has to be *sold*. And it isn't easy to do so, because great work is unexpected. It's often unlike anything the client has seen before. It's risky, bold, and daring. It's easy to sell mediocre work. Mediocre work is expected, looks just like most of the other work in the category, won't get anyone fired (at least not right away), and is, most of all, safe.

If you want to do safe work, read no further. But if you want to do great work, learn how to sell it.

The secret to selling great work is to sell the *idea* of the work before you sell the work.

Your audience hasn't been thinking about the problem you've solved nearly as long as you have. They just understand the problem. So you've got to get them to where you are by using emotion and enthusiasm, but delivered in a *logical* progression. You've got to sell them on the *idea* before they will buy the execution. The aim is to avoid jump balls or 50/50 balls, or any discussion that could derail your argument. Don't rely on your audience's taste or judgment. Frame your argument in such a way that you *eliminate possible solutions until the only solution possible is yours.* Then show it.

Let me give you an example from one of our student projects. If kids in grad school can do this, you can, too.

This example is from a presentation of creative work for a manufacturer of hockey equipment. I'm not going to use the real brand names here to avoid any legal issues. The names aren't important. The ideas are.

I'm going to paraphrase because I can't recall the exact words used, but once again, the ideas are what's important. The manufacturer's representatives weren't in the room, but let's pretend they were just so you understand framing.

The leader of the student team stood up and began, "You gentlemen make remarkable hockey equipment. The leather in your skates is of the finest quality, supple yet strong. The blades on the skates are sharp and perfectly aligned. Your sticks are made of the finest composites for maximum strength and flexibility. It probably seems like a good idea to tell your potential customers about all this. But there's just one problem—that's exactly what Brand XXX is doing. They got there first and there's no point in saying the same thing as them. And besides, we're not a 'me too' brand. But what *can* we say about us?"

"I grew up playing hockey in northern Michigan, like most American and Canadian kids in that thin strip of land that encompasses the border of Canada and the United States and runs from New England to British Columbia. Probably like you guys." *Now they are nodding.*

"And we didn't play indoors on rinks, we played outdoors on frozen ponds."

*More nodding.*

"We played all day outside every chance we got. Whether there were two of us or twelve, we didn't care, we just wanted to play hockey."

*More nodding.*

"And the thing I remember most about those days was how cold it was.

"It was really cold. But that didn't stop us. We kept playing. We'd check one another into snow banks. We'd get soaking wet. And then it was even colder. But we didn't care, because we loved hockey."

*A lot more nodding.*

"And anybody who loves hockey knows that feeling. The feeling of being really cold, but not caring because you love playing so much. That's the soul of hockey. That's what it's all about—the cold."

*A lot more nodding and smiling.*

"What if we could own the cold?"

At which point he unveiled a spread magazine ad with a beautiful photograph of a frozen pond, the brand's logo in the lower right-hand corner, and the headline, "Ah, 22 Below."

He then showed them two more executions on the same theme. Lots of nodding and hand shaking all around. Success. A sold campaign.

But can you imagine what would have happened had he just walked into the room and placed on the table an ad for hockey equipment with no equipment in the ad and just a photo of a frozen pond and the headline, "Ah, 22 Below"?

He would not have sold the work. He might have been thrown out of the room. If he was really their agency, he might have been fired.

Same work, different approach. He *framed* the argument. He eliminated the obvious solution and took the audience by the hand, leading them to a point where the only possible solution had to be his.

Sell the idea of the work, then sell the work.

## THE EMOTIONAL ARCHAEOLOGIST

The most popular television series in the history of public broadcasting is Ken Burns's *The Civil War.* The show first aired in September 1990. It became a national phenomenon. More people watched all or part of this eleven-hour series than any public broadcasting show before, or since. It spawned a book. A boxed set of videos. And was repeated over and over. It generated millions of dollars, and is largely credited with making public broadcasting viable during a difficult time. It won Ken Burns countless awards and the license to continue to make whatever programs he wished.

But why? Why was the show so hugely successful? Thousands of books had been written about the Civil War. Hundreds of films and television shows of all descriptions had mined the War Between the States. Most of us had spent hours studying this terrible conflict in school. So why did it capture us so?

If, in early 1990, you had conducted a poll among the American people and asked them, "About what subject would you like to see an eleven-hour television series, consisting almost entirely of still photographs and mostly in black and white, presented on consecutive nights on your public broadcasting channel?" I doubt that they would have responded, "The Civil War." In fact, I doubt that they would have responded with any subject. What an outrageous prospect. Eleven hours about anything is beyond the imagination of most of us. Let alone the Civil War. Yet, the audience for the show grew every night.

Why?

Because Ken Burns found a way to make the Civil War an emotional experience for his viewers. He found a way to articulate the events of that bloody conflict in such a way that we all could empathize. We all could feel what it must have been like to have fought in the war, or to have waited at home for the return of our loved ones. He used the actual words of the participants, via some of the most beautiful writing ever put to paper, to bring those days to life. We looked into the eyes of a young Union soldier as the narrator read the words he had written to his wife the day before he died. We heard the fiery speeches of the abolitionists. The terse reports from the front. All accompanied by a spare, haunting arrangement of music from the period.

Ken Burns touched us. He took four years of history, compressed it to eleven hours, and made America hang on every word. He tapped that collective unconscious. He touched that place inside of all of us, regardless of who we are, or where we come from. And the key was emotion.

In an interview, when asked how he would describe himself, Ken Burns did not answer "film maker." Or historian, or author, or director. He called himself "an emotional archaeologist." What a beautiful way to describe his skill. I think the lesson here is clear. Whatever the subject matter, there is a way to make it meaningful and relevant to our audience. There is a way to capture our audience's imagination, and persuade them to our point of view. That way is through the use of emotion.

On several occasions during my career I did such a good job of creating an emotional charge in the room that I became caught up in it as well. What I was saying moved several people to tears, and caused me to choke up while speaking. It's not a technique, it's not something you can summon up, it just happens. And when it does, it's very powerful. Here's Mike Hughes, one of the most successful creative leaders in the business, with his thoughts on the subject:

*I was honored to be invited to speak at a university's commencement. I sometimes give talks that are (to me, at least) pretty emotional. I often get choked up. I hate it when it happens, but it happens. As we were waiting to enter the auditorium, one of the deans, who is a friend of my friend Harry, started chatting with me. "Have you ever spoken to a live audience of five to six thousand people?" "Um . . . no." "Boy you must be really nervous. I know I'd be really nervous." "Well, I hadn't been, but now that you mention it. . . ." "And Harry tells me you often cry when you're speaking. Are you going to cry this time?" Yikes.*

*The talk itself went fine. In fact, I got what I was told was a very rare standing ovation. I wasn't at all nervous. I didn't cry once. (OK, once I got a little choked up, but that's not crying.) At the time, I thought the dean was being a little cavalier about my pre-talk jitters, but maybe it helped me bring focus to my talk. I still wish he hadn't done it.*

**—Mike Hughes, president, The Martin Agency**

# FIVE

## HOW TO BE

I n chapter 3 we discussed the importance of the attitude that we present to our audience. So it's natural to ask, "What should that attitude be?" Or, more to the point, "How should I be?"

We're going to answer that, but before we do, we've got to deal with something I encounter in my students almost every single day—fear.

In public opinion polls, when asked their greatest personal fear, Americans rank public speaking as number one. Number one, ahead of death. That's pretty amazing when you first think about it, but after a while it begins to make some sense. We're all afraid of embarrassing ourselves in front of a group of people, of making such fools of ourselves that we'll never live it down. Of being naked while the whole world is wearing clothes. Whereas we can go off quietly by ourselves and die. No one even has to be around. It's simple, it's just over. But speaking in front of a group of other human beings—now that's truly terrifying. I really don't mean to be flip about a subject as weighty as dying, but that's what the research indicates. I guess that may be where the term "a fate worse than death" originated.

I had a student some years ago who felt that way. I asked her, "Do you mean to say you would really rather die than do this presentation?" To which she answered, "Yes." She said she wasn't kidding. That it was really that hard for her. This was puzzling to me because she was a really smart, very attractive woman. If you were to meet her for the first time, you would assume that she was a very confident person. I asked her what happened to her when she got up to speak. She said that her vision began to cloud over, becoming increasingly like a white, milky glow that narrowed her field of vision gradually to the point that all she could see was white. Wow. I made her present anyway. The only way to deal with this fear is to take it head-on.

We tried everything we could think of to help her get over this.

Finally, she came up with the answer. The way that she was able to speak in front of the class was to sit on the floor and invite everyone else to do the same. For some reason, this did the trick. The white, milky glow began to recede to the point where at the end of the semester, she was standing in front of the room on her own two feet. She had, of course, cured herself.

Fear manifests itself in strange ways. Not long ago, I was sitting down with a creative director from one of my workshops to look at his individual presentations on the DVD that we had recorded. This was a guy who also claimed to be terrified at getting up to speak. So in one of his presentations, I had allowed him to present while sitting in a chair. At one point in his presentation, he had become so enthusiastic about the idea he was presenting that he jumped up from his chair and began to move around the room, excitedly explaining his idea. When he was finished, he returned to his seat. But when we watched the performance together on DVD, he had no recollection of even getting up. "None?" "None. I don't remember anything about it at all."

But seeing himself was powerful medicine. He watched it together with me several times. Gradually, he began to see that he could do this without falling on his face. That he could communicate successfully. I won't say that he became the best presenter in his agency overnight, because he didn't. But he was now able to get up with his partner and persuade his audience that his ideas were good for them.

What causes this fear? From what I can tell, it's driven by at least four things—Feeling Safe, Being Right, Feeling Good, and Looking Good.

If any of these conditions are challenged, we become fearful. And in most peoples' minds, presentations are an opportunity to hit the Grand Slam—Not Feeling Safe, Not Being Right, Not Feeling Good, and definitely Not Looking Good.

We can all learn to become more effective presenters. We can learn to develop enough confidence to stand up and say what's on our mind. To become more effective communicators. To persuade our audience—whether it's one person or one thousand—to our point of view.

## BE YOURSELF. EVERYONE ELSE IS TAKEN.

The key to that is learning to accept one critical precept—the answer lies within ourselves. No, grasshopper, this is not a Zen approach to presenting, it's simply the conclusion that I've come to after thirty years and thousands of presentations. **There is no one right way.** Any more than there is one right way to sing a song. Or swing at a golf ball. I know that there are people out there who will tell you otherwise. Organizations that make a good deal of money teaching people exactly how to behave in order to be a better presenter. I just don't buy it. Let me put it this way. Would we find it entertaining if every professional singer tried to sing exactly like Frank Sinatra? I don't think so. We like variety. We like differences. Some of us even like quirkiness. We would grow very tired of listening to one singer after another doing Ol' Blue Eyes. To the point where singing wouldn't even be a form of entertainment anymore. Maybe that seems like a particularly extreme example to you, but is it any crazier than telling everyone that they should present in exactly the same way?

That they should stand in a certain posture, holding their arms and hands at a particular angle, and affect a certain attitude, emphasizing certain words, speaking at a certain volume, pausing at all the same points, and all while very cunningly dressing for success? No, it just doesn't make any sense.

Which is why I've never told anyone, "Stand like a Pirate." But that's essentially what some people who claim to know what they're doing tell their students.

There was only one Frank Sinatra. There's only one Jon Steel, or Jeff Goodby, or John Adams. They're very, very good at what they do. They're very, very good presenters. But that doesn't mean we should model ourselves after them. They each possess much to emulate, and much to learn from. But maybe the most important thing to learn is that each of them has their own distinct style. Each of which is highly effective. In their own way. None of them tries to be someone they're not. Why, therefore, should we as lesser mortals attempt to be someone we are not? Of course we shouldn't. The simple truth of the matter is that each of us has it within us to be the very best us we can be. The best Bob Smith, or Sally Jones. No one is as good at being you as you.

We all have attributes that are just waiting to be used. We only have to summon up the confidence to use them. To get it through our heads once and for all that it isn't necessary to be like some great speaker we saw at a conference or on television. In fact, it would be a mistake. Because isn't a big part of what we liked about that speaker the fact that she was unique? That we hadn't seen anybody quite like her before? That there was just something about the way she took control of the audience, knew what she was talking about, and delivered her message effectively?

> **TAKE NOTE**
>
> According to scientists, the physiological changes that occur in humans when they are afraid and when they are excited are identical. So the way we feel and the way we appear to the audience are exactly the same when we're afraid and when we're excited.

So why not choose to be excited? Actually, the way to deal with those nervous feelings is to channel them into adrenalin. Let the feelings pump you up. Enjoy the feeling of being excited.

In every workshop and class I have conducted for the past ten years, someone will finish their presentation, return to their seat, and claim that they were terrified. Each time, I ask the audience if the presenter appeared to be terrified. And every single time, the answer is "No." We don't appear to be afraid, we just appear to be excited.

We need to understand this—the feelings of nervousness that we are experiencing simply do not transmit to the audience to anywhere near the degree with which we feel them. That's a long way of saying the audience can't tell that we're nervous.

Unless we're holding a flimsy piece of paper and our hand is shaking like a leaf. If you tend to shake, don't hold paper. Have it mounted on foam core or let someone else hold the paper.

The process of figuring out your individual style can take some time and a lot of practice. Take every opportunity you can find to present. Internally, at your workplace, perhaps at organizations outside work where you may volunteer, or even at Toastmasters. Most cities in North America have multiple Toastmasters Clubs. The purpose of the clubs is to bring professionals together on a regular basis and have the members present to one another. It's designed to help you become better, and a lot of people have benefited from it.

The most effective tool you can use is video. You can get help from a friend, or you can even do it by yourself. Today's lightweight video cameras have excellent quality and are easy to use. You can even use your phone.

Get into a room and record yourself delivering a presentation that you have prepared. Look at the playback. Are you happy with it? Does the person in the video resemble anyone you know? Many times, my students are shocked to see and hear themselves. Not just because we all think we need to lose weight, but because without seeing ourselves, we have a hard time realizing what impression we are delivering when we stand up in front of the room to present.

Analyze your performance. If you're coming off as too stiff, or too "professional," loosen it up. You might even ask a friend to take a look and share her thoughts with you.

Then do it again. And again. It takes hard work.

But over time, you will begin to see what works for you and what doesn't.

If you're naturally funny, being humorous will work, but that has to be tempered. If you're very good at delivering a quiet emotional message, then try that style.

Some people really benefit by moving around the room. Others are more comfortable standing in one place.

Try different things. Keep experimenting. Eventually, you will discover what works for you.

Once you've arrived at a style, stay with it. Don't change it. Of course, if you are talking about a specific subject, you will tailor your delivery to an attitude that is appropriate to the subject. Likewise, if you're in a huge room at a convention center, you'll address the audience differently than if you were in someone's office. But don't change your style. It's what makes you—you. And that's what we're after.

## KNOW EVERYBODY'S "STUFF"

The surest defense against nerves is this—know your stuff.

Nothing will cure as many presentation ills as knowing your stuff.

And by "your stuff," I don't just mean your part of the presentation. If you are presenting with teammates—and that's the way the vast majority of presentations go down today—know *everybody's* part. Know the entire presentation.

You may have to bail out a teammate who forgets an important point. If you don't know the point she was going to make, you can't bail her out, can you? And by the way, if what she forgets to say isn't critical to the idea you're trying to sell, let it go. It's better to just move on and not look like you guys don't know what you're doing, or that you are somehow undermining your teammate by pointing out that she missed something. Audiences hate the appearance of dissidence within a team. They run from it. So **when you are presenting as a team, at least *act* as if you like one another.**

Suppose your teammate doesn't make the plane? Literally. It's happened thousands of times. You've got to be able to stand up and deliver her part. So you better know it.

But even more importantly, there may be a time during the presentation when things don't go exactly as planned. Maybe the client says, "Look, we already know all about that, what we want to hear about is what you're going to do about it." You'd better be able to adjust what you rehearsed and deliver what the client needs. The entire team has to be so well prepared and know the material so well that they can switch on the fly to cover something that they hadn't planned on doing.

VCU Brandcenter students learn this lesson early in their first year at school in Professor Don Just's class, "The Business of Branding." Don assigns a team of five a case study to be presented one week hence. The day of the presentation all five are there, ready to go. Don gets them all pumped up, and then tells two of them to sit down. "You missed the plane, and your wife had a baby. You two didn't make the trip. You three do the presentation." The rest of the class gets the idea very quickly.

Knowing the material will fix whatever ails you, but more than anything, it will eliminate one of the major reasons for fear—

fear of forgetting what you're supposed to say. You won't forget, because you know it.

Notice I say "know it." Do not memorize. That will lead you to trouble. You will forget a key word from one of the sentences that you memorize. And you won't be able to move on with the presentation, because you don't really know the material, you only know the words you memorized. It may as well be in French. And now you're stuck, *mon ami*. It happens all the time. I see people rummaging around in their memory for that perfect word or phrase that they "memorized." Only they really didn't.

Also, memorizing typically comes off exactly like memorizing. It appears that the speaker is repeating what he memorized. So it's stiff and unnatural.

Watch a good actor sometime. He appears to be saying what has just occurred to him. He's expressing an idea. A bad actor appears to be repeating what he memorized. It doesn't seem in any way genuine.

So don't memorize. Know the material. Make it yours. And then deliver it in your words and your own style with CLARITY, CONVICTION, AND GRACE.

Here's Darren Moran describing his personal style:

*By solving one of my greatest presentation weaknesses, Peter inadvertently created my unique style of presenting. Like 98 percent of the rest of the world, I had a nasty habit of filling the empty spaces between the actual words of my presentations with "ummms." Peter beat that out of me pretty quickly.*

*But what he couldn't solve was my terrible memory. No matter how hard I try, I just can't memorize speeches or presentations. When I know the material I'm presenting well . . . when I'm in my comfort zone . . . it flows fine. But when presenting new material or ideas, I have to search my mind for what I was planning to say next to actually create a coherent presentation. And that searching sometimes takes time. Absent the "ummms," this situation creates long silences, abruptly punctuated by a rapid-fire patter. Rather than sounding hesitant or unsure, it has the curious effect of making it seem like I'm pausing for very, very dramatic effect, inveighing even the lowliest conjunction with incredible importance. The cycle of hitting the brake every time I get up to 60, then stepping on the gas again after sitting idle gives my presentations an eerily similar quality to a NYC cab ride: you may not always enjoy the journey, but you'll never fall asleep, and you'll be thrilled to arrive in one piece at the end.*

—Darren Moran, executive creative director, DraftFCB

## THE THIN LINE

In trying to explain to people how to do this thing called presenting, how to do it without fear, I grasp for whatever it is that connects with that particular student. Different people respond to different stimuli, and if I'm not careful, I can cause someone to adopt a persona that really isn't them. We quickly solve that problem, but it has caused me to realize how delicate the balance is between one persona that is perfectly effective and one that is ineffective.

For example, it's become clear to me is that there is a fine line between confidence and arrogance. It is critical that we not only be confident, but that we project that confidence. It doesn't do us much good if we feel confident but appear to be nervous, or unsure of ourselves, or distracted, or any of a thousand other not so useful things. Remember, people tend to believe what they see, so if we're confident (and we'd better be), then we need to project that confidence.

So we're confident and we project it. But we don't want to cross that fine line between confidence and arrogance. It's easy to do. And once you've done it, it isn't easy to come back. Your audience will most likely have dismissed you as a jerk by then. Most people will catch themselves before they've gone too far, but I've seen more than one presenter turn himself into a game show host. It isn't pretty.

Then we've got the guy who is good at presenting. But maybe a little too "good." "What now?" you're wondering. This book is all about becoming a great presenter, and he's complaining about someone being "too good?" Let me explain. It isn't unusual for me to encounter a presenter who is confident in his ability, knows his stuff, and has been very successful in the past. At least, in his own mind. What he doesn't realize is that what he thinks of as "polished," is actually coming off as "slick." Audiences don't like "slick." "Slick" is a synonym for "inauthentic." And "inauthentic" really is deadly. So it's got to be stamped out.

This is, as you might expect, rather unpleasant for me as the facilitator of the workshop, and usually less so for the slick guy.

Here's a guy who's doing all the stuff I've been talking about, he's just doing too much of it in too "big" a way. The audience knows it. If I don't call him out on it, I lose credibility with the workshop. I try to be as positive as possible in my comments, but I do the guy a disservice if I don't call him out. So I do. I first had to do that many years ago with a gentleman who was part of the top management team at the agency I was working with. He was the most senior guy in the room.

He thought that all of the junior folks in the room admired his sterling presentation abilities. He didn't realize that they thought he was a fraud. Difficult stuff. The easy thing would have been to compliment him and move on. But I wouldn't really have been helping him if I had, and I'd have lost the respect of everyone else in the room at the same time.

So, with some trepidation, I brought up the idea of him being "too good." At first he was taken aback, but slowly he began to get the idea. I have always insisted on video recording every presentation by every participant, but up until that day I hadn't been doing private, one-on-one analyses of each participant's video. Once this gentleman and I were able to look at his video and talk about it in private, he really appreciated what I had been saying and determined to adjust his performances accordingly. He would be confident, just not "too confident."

It's interesting that we are drawn to confidence. We follow confident people. But turn the confidence dial up a little too high, and the audience is turned off.

The way I usually describe the presenter who's crossed over the line is as "a game show host." You know how those guys are inevitably smarmy, oily, slick, self-absorbed, sometimes even condescending? They think they're funny, so they laugh at their own jokes. They make facial expressions worthy of a silent film actor. They don't pay any attention to what anyone else in the room is saying or thinking. Don't be that guy. Almost no one I work with is capable of turning into the "game show host," but by being aware of the possibility, they are assured that they will not.

Which is why, I think, a little self-deprecating humor goes a long way.

*"No one likes a perfect creative director."*

*I think most creative directors would agree with that statement. Yet most creative directors (including myself) approach a presentation with the desire to make ourselves look perfect. Our delivery. Our ideas. Our jokes. I guess it's just natural instinct that we believe the clients want us to be "perfect."*

*But I think if you can find some simple ways to make yourself more human—more imperfect—then there is a better chance of warming up clients. And at least building a little empathy before presenting these great ideas you've worked so hard to polish into perfection.*

*So here's one little trick I've used over the last year or two that I think has helped in some meetings and pitches. Before showing the final work, I quickly (very quickly) touch on the creative process of getting to this work. I start by explaining how "the creative teams really had fun exploring a lot of options." (Then I click to a slide showing quick unposed shots of teams working and typing. This simple slide says there are human beings behind these ideas.) Then I say, "And after a week or so, there were a ton of options and ways at this strategy." (Then I click to a photo or two of a giant long wall filled with papers and scraps. I even show a tight shot of something crude or a bad drawing. It's best to show the true ugliness and raw nature of a wall like this. Showing a wall filled with imperfection says a lot about the open-mindedness of the CD presenting.) And then I will follow that by saying, "But ultimately we had to edit all of this down and get to the work that really hits our strategy." (At this point, I click to a slide that shows a few photos of work lying all over the floor, in the trash, under tables. These are real scenes every day in a creative department, so capture them along the way with a little phone camera. And by showing this death all over the floor, the CD is kind of saying that it's OK to kill ideas. That visual statement is comforting to clients. They are more receptive to buying an idea when they start knowing that it's OK to kill an idea.)*

*In the end, I've found that if the images are truly authentic, then you have a chance to convey yourself and the creative department as imperfect. And that's a great place to begin the process of selling work.*

**—Chris Jacobs, executive creative director, Cramer-Krasselt**

## HUMOR VS. JOKES

Most of us have a sense of humor. We may not be the funniest people in the world, but we've got a sense of humor. We use it to great effect in our lives, helping us to make points, soften the impact of bad news, or simply helping people see who we are—and like us.

Yet when it comes time to give a presentation, many of us decide to unplug that sense of humor. Because this is a professional situation and it calls for Professional Behavior. Right? Yes, but it doesn't mean that we shouldn't be funny or humorous. It doesn't mean that we shouldn't use our natural sense of humor.

And one of the best ways to do that, to humanize ourselves, if you will, is to be self-deprecating. People like people who don't take themselves too seriously. We should take what we do seriously, and what we're there to talk about in the presentation is doubtless a serious subject, but we can still show that we aren't overly impressed with ourselves by being self-deprecating from time to time. Don't overdo it, though. You want them to think you're modest, not incompetent.

Humor can play a major role in making the emotional connection that we're striving for.

The people in your audience use the left side of the brain, the analytical side, to rationalize decisions, but they make decisions with the right side, the emotional, intuitive side. So use your sense of humor. Being funny is great, but what we should not do, under any circumstances, is tell jokes.

The humor we use should come from real-life situations. This can be an incident that occurred in the room before you went on, or a funny thing that happened while you guys were putting together the presentation. It can be a funny story about one of your colleagues, or something funny you heard about the subject you're discussing.

It's the way in which you tell a story or make a point that can be funny. For example, when I'm demonstrating eye contact for workshop groups, I often use the following demonstration.

When you were in school, your teacher may have told you to just look at the back wall of the room and everyone in the room will think you're looking at them. I say this while staring at the back wall. I then ask, "Does anyone think I'm looking at them?" Of course, no one does, and they laugh every time. Okay, it's not the funniest story in the world, but it makes the point in a humorous way.

## THOUGHTFULNESS

In one of the more bizarre chapters in my New Business Presentation experience, our agency presented for a large business-to-business account on a stage in front of a large live audience. It was like something out of a television show. The company's auditorium was full of people watching the competing agencies present and, from time to time, an audience member would wander up to the stage and snap a photo or two. The CMO of the company had decided that he wanted to open up the process to anyone in the company who was interested. So he invited all the employees. But he didn't stop there. At that time in the Washington, D.C., Metro area, there was a very popular business magazine called *Regardie's*. The CMO invited a writer from the magazine to sit in on all the presentations and do a story based on what he saw and heard.

The CMO asked if we would object to having a reporter in the room. We said we didn't since he was determined to have the guy there anyway.

This was the kind of situation that many people would have found paralyzing. "Oh my God, not only do we have to present in front of a theater-size audience, we have to do it in front of a reporter who's going to write about how horrible we are. Oh my God, Oh my God."

You probably won't be surprised to hear that we didn't feel that way. I thought it was a very interesting wrinkle and just maybe an opportunity for some great publicity about our agency. The bottom line was this—I knew that we had a great presentation and that I really knew the material. So I wasn't afraid.

As it turned out, we won. And it was a great PR opportunity. *Regardie's* ran a major story on the presentations, with particular emphasis on ours. They even ran a photo of my partner and me on the cover. It was really cool.

But there was one aspect of the piece that I found more than a bit disturbing. In describing my partner and me, he characterized him as "the more thoughtful of the two." That really stung. I later asked the writer about it, and he claimed that "Well, you do all the talking up there on the stage, in front of everybody, and you're like the star of the show, and he doesn't ever say much and takes his time before he says anything."

Well, it was true that we had won and that, as I said, I did all the talking. But in the interview that accompanied the article, my partner and I took turns answering the writer's questions. In fact, I deferred a bit to my partner because I wanted him to have a piece of the spotlight as well.

The writer went on to say that he was really trying to build up my partner and meant no disrespect to me, but I took it very seriously indeed.

Never appear to be anything but thoughtful. Thoughtfulness is one of the most important attributes we can possess. Particularly in new business and client meetings. This is extremely important for young people. If you appear to be young, people may assume that you are inexperienced, less than savvy, and not really in any position to be telling folks what to do. But all of that can be overcome if you appear to be thoughtful. Choose your language carefully. Don't come off as someone on a reality television show sitting in a hot tub. Use a vocabulary of achievement and victory. The words you choose, and how you deliver them, say a lot about you and your organization. Say things once and say them with power. Don't appear glib. Don't answer too quickly. Take your time and answer in measured sentences. Don't diminish yourself because you're the most junior person in the room. You've learned a lot in your time. Think of it as being wise beyond your years. And be thoughtful.

Please understand, I'm not talking about writing thank you notes or being considerate of others. Although that secondary definition of "thoughtful" is very important and I believe in it completely.

I'm talking about the quality that certain people seem to have that communicates intelligence. Wisdom. Knowing your stuff. It's not necessary to do a lot of talking in a meeting or presentation to seem thoughtful. It is only necessary that the things you say are smart. Insightful. Cogent. Even brave. And if you're really good at it, your ideas will be so thoughtful, and so well expressed, that they can't be refuted.

Mike Hughes of The Martin Agency once said, "The four things clients want the most are Insight, Conviction, Wisdom, and Courage." Notice Mike didn't mention cool ads. Which isn't to say he doesn't believe in them, because he certainly does, but he was explaining the things that are most important to clients. And Mike knows that if the client doesn't think those four key attributes are present in his agency, and in the people who work on his business, there probably won't be any cool ads done anytime soon.

The key to communicating those key attributes is thoughtfulness. Clients want to work with smart people who care about their business. Not people who want to do cool ads. So it is critical that we present ourselves in a thoughtful way. That our arguments are structured in a precise, logical manner. And that each statement, while built on the last, leads into the next. Segues are critical.

Non sequiturs, verboten.

This isn't to say that you've got to come off like a Harvard B-School professor. This doesn't mean that you should be boring. Quite the contrary. You should be inspirational. Use all the creativity you're planning on putting into those cool ads to win over your prospect/client. Because unless you win them over, no cool ads.

From time to time, I'm asked to help a client find the right ad agency for them. One of the most exciting moments for me in that process is encountering someone who has a fresh take on things, a point of view I haven't heard before, or even a new way of talking about stuff I have heard before. Those are the kind of people I try to get in front of my client, the new business prospect. Because those are the kind of people who I believe the prospect deserves to meet.

Those are the kind of people I would describe as thoughtful.

Those are the kind of people who stand out from the crowd and win.

## THE WAY WE SAY THINGS

Let me give you an example of a team of presenters distinguishing themselves from the competition.

For a couple of years, The Martin Agency operated an internal training program called The Martin Workshop. They asked me to organize the program. With a lot of help from other folks, we managed to put together a six-month program covering all the essentials that anyone would need to master in order to succeed at The Martin Agency, or at any agency, for that matter.

The young folks chosen to participate in the program were recommended by their supervisors as "rising stars." They came from every department and discipline within the agency and they were an impressive group, to say the least.

At the end of the six-month "semester," the participants were split into two teams and asked to develop a Communications Plan for an actual agency client and present it to a panel of judges. The panel was made up of the top management of the agency, and representatives of the client would often come to see the show as well. Needless to say, this was a wonderful opportunity for the teams to strut their stuff in front of folks to whom they would normally have very limited, if any, access. Throw in the presence of actual clients, and you've got a crucible of anxiety that is about as close to real life as you can come.

I was involved with the program for three or four "semesters," and the winning team in these competitions was always the team that gave the best presentation. Not the team with what might be called the "best ideas," but the team that presented their ideas the best. And that is almost always the way it is. Everywhere. All the time.

Why? Because no one knows if one idea is better than another if it isn't presented in such a way that it is clear to the audience that the idea is better.

**TAKE NOTE**

William Goldman, the noted screenwriter and novelist (*Butch Cassidy and the Sundance Kid, Marathon Man, The Princess Bride*) wrote a wonderful book about Hollywood called *Adventures in the Screen Trade: A Personal View of Hollywood and Screenwriting,* in which he adamantly proclaims that "no one in Hollywood knows anything." What he means by this is that no one—studio heads, producers, directors, writers, agents, actors—none of them have any idea what will be successful in the marketplace and what will not. That's why we see so many expensive failures and surprising small films succeed. That's really why we see the same ideas over and over, to the point where the safest films to produce are sequels nearly identical to their predecessors.

The same can be said about advertising. No one knows anything. Oh, there are certain obvious "rules" about good design and writing, and lots of people think they know a good strategy when they see one, but the truth of the matter is, this is a subjective activity. It usually boils down to whose opinion is the most powerful in the room. Clients have an opinion and the agency has an opinion. Sometimes, they can reach an accord. A lot of the time, they can't.

I see this subjectivity demonstrated time and again at our school. A student can take an idea to one professor and get a very well-reasoned opinion on the work. That student can then take that same idea next door to the office of another professor and get another very well-reasoned opinion that is completely opposite from that of the first professor. Neither one of them is wrong.

*(continues)*

But the truth is that no one in advertising, as in the film industry, really knows what will work in the marketplace. We can make some pretty good educated guesses, but we can't be sure. Which is why so much of the work produced by advertising agencies is tested before it runs. This could lead to another long rant, so I'll stop with the digression now. Just remember that it's all subjective.

The last competition at The Martin Workshop that I was involved in brought that notion into even higher relief. There were two teams involved in the "finals." Both groups worked completely independently, although they received the same briefing from the actual account supervisor who worked on the account for The Martin Agency.

In their presentations, both groups presented *virtually identical* ideas. Yet one group was unanimously chosen as the winner. In the deliberations with the panel of judges prior to rendering the decision, several judges pointed out the "great ideas" that the winning team offered, *although the other team presented exactly the same ideas.* How can this be? It's simple, and as I said earlier, it happens all the time. The winning team presented their ideas with language that was colorful, powerful, unusual, even exciting. Their vocabulary, as presented orally and in their PowerPoint slides, was markedly different from that of the runners-up. Their choice of words was thoughtful and action oriented, and their ideas were presented with a creative flair that was lacking in the other team's presentation. And it was that choice of vocabulary used to describe their ideas and their approach to problem solving that so distinguished their work from that of their competitors that day.

Here's an important point I want to make: while it's true that the audience will likely remember less than 10 percent of what you say orally, you must give them exciting and powerful words to hang onto. If they only remember a few, make them great.

And don't forget that, even though they will forget much of what you say, they will remember what *they* thought about what *you* said. So be sure to make them think.

I'm convinced that that's what happened in the minds of the judges that day at The Martin Agency. The judges remembered what they thought and how they felt when they were listening to the presentation. Everything they heard and saw made an impression—or it didn't.

Always remember that the way in which we present our ideas is every bit as important, if not *more* important, than the ideas themselves. When we are selling our ideas, the audience must first buy *us*.

And as we said earlier, if we want them to buy "us," we have to show them who "us" really is. Not some caricature of "us," but the genuine article. Because it is this genuine representation of ourselves that our audience will find authentic. And authenticity is what we seek.

Authenticity comes from the heart. Find what not just you, but the *team* believes in its heart. And tell your truth.

*The Volkswagen of America pitch was the most memorable pitch I have been involved with. Arnold was the dark horse. We felt like underdogs. USA Today was following Donny Deutsch around during the pitch and we were this cobbled-together agency in Boston. My creative partner at the time, Alan Pafenbach, and I raised our hands. I had owned many VWs over the years and felt like I knew what made them so special to their owners. We were both the target market, so to speak.*

*They were coming into town to visit the agency, and we thought we would make a video. Alan and I went down to the bar below the agency and the first thing we wrote down, on a napkin no less, was that on the road of life there are passengers and there are drivers. We wrote a bunch more lines, which eventually became the TV spots, pretty fast.*

*That weekend we drove around in my Jetta with my friend Joe Fallon, who has since become a writer and creative director who we hired at Arnold. We basically just acted like we always do, having stupid conversations in cars. Not slick at all.*

*We cut that footage into whatever else we could find and put music we liked on it the night before they arrived and played it for them the next day. We learned later that we basically won the account right then. Of course, we didn't know that at the time and spent the next month trying to get all clever. Ron Lawner kept pushing us back to the spirit of the video. He wrote the words "Drivers wanted" and stuck it up on the wall, and that was that.*

*On the road of life, there are passengers, and there are drivers. Drivers wanted.*

*The words looked good next to the logo.*

*This was the first really big pitch I was ever involved with. We were all very, very nervous. I wore a suit. The clients asked if it was the same suit I got married in. It was. They cracked up. And that put everyone at ease. I asked if they were at the wedding. I guess it was obvious I wasn't a suit-and-tie kind of guy.*

*We had all the pitch work-up on black walls behind us. We had the words set big, above all the work.*

*Kristen Volk, the planner, recovered fast when the power went out because someone kicked the cord out of the laptop or something. She knew her stuff, so it didn't matter, and I think the clients appreciated the human aspect of that. We all just spoke from the heart, the words just poured out. We were a team that spoke in one voice. We really did believe that we had captured the spirit of VW. Still, I couldn't believe it when Ron called me and told me the news.*

*It was the largest account ever won by a New England ad agency at the time.*

**—Lance Jensen, executive creative director, Hill Holliday**

# SIX

# AUTHENTICITY

"There is a vitality, a life force, an energy, a quickening that is translated through you into action, and because there is only one of you in all of time, this expression is unique. And if you block it, it will never exist through any other medium and it will be lost."

—*Martha Graham, pioneer of modern dance*[1]

Certain presenters seem to win all the time. They seem to always get what they want. Why is that? Are they smarter than everybody else? Are they just "better presenters?" Are their agencies just better?

In a few cases, the answer to all three of these questions is "Yes." But it isn't always the case, and even when it is, that isn't the real reason certain presenters always win.

A handful of presenters always seem to win because they have mastered one important skill. They have learned how to be authentic. The dictionary defines "authentic" as "of undisputed origin;

genuine. Made or done in the traditional or original way, or in a way that faithfully resembles an original."

My *New Oxford American Dictionary* goes on to say "based on facts; accurate or reliable—an authentic depiction of the situation."

And an authentic depiction of the situation is characterized as *reliable, dependable, trustworthy, authoritative, honest, and faithful.*

That's why we need to be authentic. Because people believe us when we're authentic. Because people trust us when we're authentic and because people will do what we ask when we're authentic. Additionally, behaving in an "original way" is seen as authentic.

So who wouldn't want to be seen as authentic?

Okay, fine, I want to be authentic, but how do I do that?

Simple. You've already got everything you need. You. Just be yourself.

Unfortunately, this idea is completely foreign to most people. They assume that if they are to give a "presentation," well, they'll have to turn into the kind of person who gives a "presentation." They then proceed to try to do an impression of whoever they see in their mind's eye as the kind of person who gives "presentations."

As we said earlier, this is exactly the wrong choice. It causes us to behave in an unnatural way, striving to emulate some model presenter who we've conjured up for the purposes of the presentation. It's hard enough to stand up in front of a room and speak as ourselves, but trying to present material as someone else, which is essentially what this amounts to, is just too much for most of us.

We're afraid to stand "naked" in front of the room, so we cloak ourselves in some phony persona. And then we compound the problem by projecting a litany of copy-heavy PowerPoint slides up on the screen, reading them verbatim to the audience, who by now has most likely checked out and is either busily checking their emails on their smartphones or wishing they could.

What we *are* good at is being ourselves. Being our authentic, down-to-earth selves. That is the only platform from which we can speak sincerely. That's the only way we're ever going to be able to build trust. And without trust, we will never accomplish anything of significance in our business relationships.

Yet people continue to believe that they have to become someone else in order to "present." In one of my workshops at Goodby, Silverstein & Partners, a broadcast producer was included in the group along with writers, art directors, account people, and planners. As we went around the room and introduced ourselves, he said that unlike his colleagues, he never really gave presentations and really didn't have any idea how to do it. Though he was happy to give it a try. I told him to not even try. Just pay attention to what we were talking about and try to apply those lessons to what he was going to do.

Of course, you can guess what happened. All he did was be himself. He spoke from the heart. He talked about his young family. He passionately explained the innovative production techniques behind a brilliant campaign for the National Basketball Association. And he charmed us all. He was the most natural presenter in the room. And therefore, the most authentic. And even though these workshops aren't competitions, he was the best.

Being who we are is powerful.

Use that power to make an emotional connection. We do that by telling our story in an authentic, emotional way. It isn't necessary to have a slick slide show or technological wonders to win an audience. In fact, those things can get in the way. And often, technology doesn't work.

What some people fear the most, being betrayed by their presentation equipment, can actually be a blessing, because it forces us to put ourselves front and center. Listen to Gareth Kay:

> *My presentation nightmare is one I'll never forget. For lots of bad reasons but also because it taught me the lesson of what really matters.*
>
> *It was my first pitch as a newly promoted board member of an agency in London called dfgw that sadly no longer exists (anything good I do in my career is mostly down to my boss there, Gary Duckworth). We were pitching a whisky brand that was trying to make itself relevant to a younger audience who saw it, literally, as "the drink my dad drinks." So we had the brilliantly (perhaps stupidly) simple strategy of doing lager ads for whisky—inject a bit of humor and sociability into an overly serious, solitary category. The ads were funny and relied on a brilliant branded mnemonic that was a catchphrase of an old English actor and comic, Leslie Phillips, who had become in-*

*credibly popular again. For the pitch we got Leslie to record this catchphrase, and idiot that I am, I decided that seeing I knew a bit about PowerPoint, I'd embed it in the charts so we could play the catchphrase throughout the presentation.*

*All went well in the rehearsals, and we ran off to the pitch at the client's brand consultancy with a laptop and some speakers. We had ten minutes to set up. The laptop powered up and then nothing. A black screen. We tried to restart. Nothing. The client arrived. Still couldn't get it started.*

*And we had no backup on another file or an external drive. All the drama had gone from the pitch. I was red in the face and angry with myself (and also probably at Bill Gates). The creative director couldn't believe we called in a favor and it was not going to be used in a big pitch.*

*That's the nightmare piece and I now tend to travel to pitches with thumb drives, backup decks in the cloud, and so forth (especially as Rich Silverstein has a reputation of being the equivalent of kryptonite to AV technology). But, despite the nightmare, it actually led to one of the best pitch performances I've ever been part of. I knew that we had no charts, just some printouts and flip charts. We knew the story we wanted to tell and I think we gave it in a more engaging, human and "loose" way than we had planned. We told stories, and to paraphrase David Ogilvy, we didn't lean on technology like a drunk leans on a lamppost, for support rather than illumination. Maybe that's an important thing for us to all remember nowadays in an*

*era where anyone can make beautiful charts and most agencies*
*rely on "shiny objects" to win—the most memorable stories are*
*the ones that are well told. By people, not presenters. And that*
*human connections are always more powerful than technologi-*
*cal fireworks.*

**—Gareth Kay, director of Brand Strategy,**
**Goodby, Silverstein & Partners**

Being who we are accelerates and enhances human connection. And that's what we're after. As we've said, we need to make a human connection—a bond that's based upon emotion. In order to make that connection, we must be honest, open, and sincere. We must show what we truly feel, not just what we believe. Human connections are emotional. The power of emotion is what binds us together and builds trust.

Without trust, we will never achieve what we want.

As I suggested in the last chapter, most people I know would never think of lying in a meeting or an interview, yet when they try to be someone they're not, they're lying, aren't they? And on some level, the audience knows it. That's why the liar loses and the authentic person wins.

Getting this thought through our heads and truly believing it is a major breakthrough for many of us. Like my art director friend in Los Angeles who learned not to be afraid to be herself, we find it powerfully liberating, because we no longer feel the strain of trying to be someone we're not, or of trying to behave in a way that is foreign to us.

I'm in no way suggesting that we behave in any way that's less than professional. We have to treat each presentation with the respect that it deserves—yes, presentations deserve respect. When we respect the presentation, when we treat it as something that's important, the audience sees that and realizes that what we're talking about is important to them. And by association, we're demonstrating that we think the audience is important as well. We've all attended presentations in which it was clear that the presenters didn't really treat the opportunity to present as significant. They're poorly prepared, their visuals are sloppy or incomplete, their thinking is mundane—and we respond negatively.

That said, while we must be professional, we don't want to be "professional." We don't want to put on our "presentation personality" and turn into the Robot Presenter from Another World.

Not long ago, I was working with a pair of executive creative directors on their presentation skills. Several of their recent presentations hadn't gone very well, and their boss suggested they get some help, which they welcomed with enthusiasm. But they really couldn't pinpoint the reason for their poor performance. Until they looked at the video recordings of the work we had been doing together earlier in the day. I always start off workshops by asking people to get up in front of the room and talk about anything they like. What they did that weekend, their kids, their hobbies—anything—but not work. We record these discussions on video. Then we record presentations from their work life. In the case of these two, we worked on the set-up and creative work from various campaigns. Then we looked at the videos. When these guys looked at the first videos, the ones in which they weren't "presenting," but were just chatting, they saw themselves. Their authentic selves. When they looked at the videos in which they were presenting work—they asked me to turn the playback machine off. Why? Because they couldn't understand the people they were looking at. Each of these guys turned into their idea of "a presenter." They were apoplectic. "I suck." "I'm terrible."

"Worst of all, I'm boring."

I asked them why they thought that was the case. They both blurted out, "I don't know who that guy is. It sure ain't me." I asked them why they changed into Presentation Robots. They said they thought that was the way they were supposed to be.

These guys aren't unique. People everywhere think that who they are isn't good enough. But when they see themselves being their true selves and then see themselves impersonating someone giving a "presentation," they get it. They change. They commit to being themselves. And at that moment, they begin to become powerful presenters. In the case of the two executive creative directors, we decided that from now on, we were going to call what they do "conversations," not "presentations."

Whatever works.

As with just about everything else in this book, I learned these lessons the hard way. The stuff I'm talking about in this book is not theoretical. It is the product of years and years of writing, designing, delivering, critiquing, and teaching presentations. With real prospects, real clients, and live ammo.

Many years ago, my agency was in the midst of a new business presentation. For some reason, we turned off the projector, turned up the lights in the room, and just started to talk with the client. This same thing happened several times before and after this particular incident, but that was usually because of some "technical difficulties." In this case, the visual aids were working just fine.

But the client asked us to turn off the projector. I can't even remember why.

What at first seemed like a disaster turned out to be a blessing. The client had done us an enormous favor and taught me a lesson that I've never forgotten.

Without the slides, which we were at least partially using as a teleprompter, we were forced to rely on our knowledge of the subject matter. We had to speak in real English as ourselves. We couldn't be "Presentation Robot." We were forced into a conversation. It was terrifying. But it was great.

He forced us into a conversation and that conversation helped him decide that he not only liked us, he trusted us and wanted to work with us.

We weren't selling, we were just having a conversation and being ourselves. Which is, of course, the best way to sell. We saw Gareth Kay's take on the subject above—if we needed more proof, here's a story from a man many people called the creative director of the decade, Alex Bogusky.

*Many years ago, we were doing a presentation comparing the low-budget stuff we were doing to this high-budget Pepsi production with Michael Jackson. Back in those days you brought ¾ inch video when you brought video so they had it in the control room ready to roll on my cue. So I opened up my talk and when I gave them the sign, they hit play and played something completely different. Apparently my people had loaded the wrong spot on the tape. As it was running, I was trying to piece together how I could use this other spot to make the same presentation and there was just no way. Sweat began to bead on my brow. The tape ended and I just decided to explain to the crowd what had happened and then act out the spot I had expected to run. That was very interactive and live and real and during the rest of the talk, it was fun to refer to the spot "that didn't run." I think that, in the end, it turned out to be a success because it got me more engaged with the audience; since then when things go wrong, I worry less and find a way to make that stuff into a positive.*

—**Alex Bogusky, activist and former chief creative officer and co-founder, CP+B**

## KNOWING WHO YOU ARE

"They know who they are."

That's what one of my clients said when I asked him what he thought about a firm with whom we had just met. It was my job to help him and his colleagues find the right firm for a particular assignment.

His assessment was right on the money. The people we met with that afternoon really did know exactly who they were, what they did, and what they didn't do. They didn't try to tailor their presentation to us, aside from showing us some case studies that seemed germane to the assignment. They didn't try to be "just what you're looking for." They were just who they were. We had met earlier with other firms that tried to be all things to all people. Whatever subject came up in the discussion, they would launch into their unique capabilities in that area. It didn't come off as credible. More importantly, it didn't seem as if they stood for anything. Or maybe that by claiming to stand for so many things, they didn't stand for any.

My clients unanimously liked the people who knew who they were. The people who had a point of view and could articulate it with clarity, conviction, and grace. They decided to hire them on the spot. And they turned out to be exactly who they said they were, exceeding my clients' already ambitious expectations.

### A Point of View

*I learned an important lesson about how not to present my first year in advertising.*

*I had just gotten a marketing degree from SMU and a job at the Richards Group in Dallas. We were pitching a giant hospital chain, and I was asked to present background research on the category to kick things off. Boy, did I kick things off. I wasn't prepared, I stuttered and stammered my way through five unintelligible minutes, and thoroughly embarrassed myself and the agency. My boss, Brad Todd, even kicked me underneath the table about halfway through. He should have punched me.*

*The lesson?*

*For me, if I don't feel strongly about the subject matter and understand it in my bones, I can't stand up in front of people and persuade them to my way of thinking. Know what you want to say. Have a point of view. Feel passionately about it. Absent that, go home.*

*Looking back, the only good that came out of the experience was it helped me decide to go to art school and give the creative side of things a go. I was a terrible account guy.*

**—Hal Curtis, creative director, Wieden & Kennedy**

We tell all of our students that they have to have a point of view. Regardless of their particular discipline, they need to bring a point of view to the table. The same goes for agencies. I believe that one of the principal reasons clients pay agencies is for their particular point of view. In fact, it really doesn't matter what business you're in—you've got to have a point of view. But you know what? Most organizations, in fact most individuals, don't have a coherent point of view about much.

Do you doubt me? Okay, ask someone a really mundane question, like "Why are you a fan of the so and so's?" They can't really tell you. Or they give you a generic, garden-variety, off-the-shelf answer. And that's the way it usually is with presentations. I can't tell you the number of times I've heard essentially the same thing from one agency after another.

Maybe that's why in an industry poll of 300 client responders, 75 percent said, "All agencies are interchangeable." In other words, three quarters of all clients believe there is no difference between ad agencies. That's staggering. What do people say about your company?

I love people who start their own companies. I particularly love people who start their own ad agencies. That's why I was delighted to meet with a group of young people who had just started a brand new agency. I really had only one question for them. "Why are you doing this?" As each of the four folks from the new agency took turns answering the question, it became clearer and clearer to all of us that the wheels were already coming off their brand new organization. None of them said anything that I hadn't heard many times before. None of them said anything particularly interesting or compelling. Most importantly, none of them said anything that made me think that they would succeed in their new enterprise. All of them are smart and very good at their particular discipline. But they lacked a true point of view or a clear vision of what was new and different and good about their company. None of them could tell me why I should be excited about their new company. Here they are, risking essentially everything they have, putting their lives on the line, and they can't articulate anything that communicates the passion they feel or the unique service they plan on delivering.

This is far from the first time I've encountered this phenomenon. I see it almost every time I'm asked to help an agency grow. Without naming names, I consulted a few years ago with an agency that had been around doing pretty good work for years. They're a group of smart, talented people. But when we sat down to analyze their brand by reviewing their promotional materials, it became apparent to me, and very quickly to them as well, that the stuff they had just didn't say anything. Oh, there were plenty of words. But no meaning. It didn't give me a reason to believe. It certainly didn't give me a reason to want to contact them if I was looking for an agency to include in a review. And, just like the young people starting their new agency, they realized right away that the stuff was just lying there on the table like a three-day-old fish. That's the really scary part. They realized that the material was terrible, but they didn't know what to do about it.

The answer? Have a point of view. Have something to say. Say it in such a way that I get excited. The key to this is the language that you use. Frame your ideas just as carefully as you would craft the copy in an ad. Have a headline. Have some body copy that supports it. And have it all stand for your brand. The expression of your brand is your point of view. It's what differentiates you from all other ad agencies. Or individuals. It's what will make your presentation stand out from all the rest.

In order to do this, you have to develop your own lexicon. Whether it's your agency talking, or just you, I suggest that you speak in your own language.

Great agencies all have their own language. Some use terms for their departments that are completely unique to their agency. Years ago, when Fallon was winning just about every new business pitch they entered, they had their own way of talking. They never used the word "advertising." Internally, the people never spoke about "advertising." Long before it was fashionable, they talked about "brands." Growing brands. The elasticity of brands. It was all about brands. And why did they do that? Because they had a point of view.

## DISCOVER YOUR CORE IDEOLOGY

All organizations should have a point of view that is based on their core purpose and core values. Some call it a mission statement, although I prefer to work with people to develop a core ideology comprised of core purpose and core values, as first delineated in Jim Collins and Jerry Porras's excellent book *Built to Last: Successful Habits of Visionary Companies*.[2] Regardless of what it's called, every organization needs to have a set of beliefs that inform everything it does.

And I mean everything. What accounts you pitch. The people you hire and fire. The kind of work you do. The way you decorate your offices. The look of your letterhead. And not least, the language that you use to express who and what you are.

Until your business decides to get serious about who it is, and why it is, and what it believes in and stands for, and finally, how it expresses itself, you will continue to struggle in the middle of that great undifferentiated pack of sameness. Your presentations will be essentially generic, wandering from one tired idea to another, with your audience unable to differentiate you from the group that went before you or the ones who came later. You'll lose a lot more than you'll win. And, maybe even worse, you'll win accounts that aren't right for you, costing you time and money and ultimately leading to hard feelings all around.

But it doesn't have to be that way. Discover who you are. No one can tell you. Look deep inside your organization to find the answer. Your people know who you are. They know what you stand for. And it usually isn't what's nicely framed and hanging in the lobby. Take that down and sit down with your people and ask them. They know.

As Collins and Porras explain in *Built to Last,* the trick is to work from the individual to the organization. The people we involve need to ask themselves,

- "What core values do you personally bring to your work?" (These should be so fundamental that you hold them regardless of whether or not they are rewarded.)

- "What would you tell your children are the core values that you hold at work and that you hope *they* will hold when they become working adults?"
- "If you awoke tomorrow morning with enough money for the rest of your life, would you continue to live those core values?"
- "Can you envision those core values being as valid for you 100 years from now as they are today?"
- "Would you continue to hold those core values even if at some point in time one or more of them became a competitive *disadvantage* ?"
- "If you were to start a new organization tomorrow in a different line of work, what core values would you build into the new organization regardless of its industry?"[3]

Those last three questions are particularly critical because they make the crucial distinction between enduring core values that should not change and business practices and strategies that should be changing all the time.

Be aware that this process probably isn't going to start and end in one pleasant three-hour meeting in the conference room. It can take months. It doesn't have to, but I've been involved in engagements that lasted for six months before the agency was satisfied that they had it right. Sometimes it happens more quickly, particularly in smaller organizations. But the premium isn't on getting it fast. It's on getting it right. It's critical that you get it right, because you're going to be living with this for the rest of your professional life. It's going to determine the direction for your business going forward. The way you present your company, the clients you seek, the people you hire, the people who quit, the decisions you make in every aspect of your business. So take the time to get it right. After all, you're not going to be changing it anytime soon.

Visit the offices of GSD&M down in Austin sometime. You'll find that their core values are carved in the floor of the atrium through which everyone enters the building every day. That's commitment. And if you talk to the former CEO, Roy Spence, you'll also find that he credits his agency's commitment to the discovery, and subsequent "living" of those core values, as the key to his agency's meteoric growth in the last fifteen years.

Pick up a copy of Roy's recent book, *It's Not What You Sell, It's What You Stand For: Why Every Extraordinary Business Is Driven by Purpose.*[4] It's all right there.

And while you're at it, buy a copy of *Built to Last* and read it. Buy copies for your key people. And begin the process. Because it's impossible to tell people who you are until you really *know* who you are.

Once you know, you can tell others. And the language you use will be your own. It will set you apart from the competition. It will be crisp and powerful. More than anything, it will reflect an uncommon thoughtfulness. And you don't have to use the word "advertising."

Maybe you didn't expect to hear a rant like that in a book about presenting, but if you aren't clear on just who and what your organization is, why should anyone care what you think about a specific issue?

# SEVEN

## DEATH BY DECK

As I travel the country visiting ad agencies and companies that have nothing to do with advertising, I encounter one alarming characteristic over and over. No matter how different the companies are, or how different the businesses they're involved in, they're all slowly but surely killing everyone they come in contact with by PowerPoint. Okay, maybe they're not killing anyone, but they are certainly boring people to within an inch of their lives.

Not long ago, I was working on presentation skills with some folks at one of the largest ad agencies in the country. I asked each of them to bring in several presentations that they had presented or would be presenting to their clients or colleagues. Every single one of them—save one—brought in their trusty laptop and fired up the PowerPoint.

These were extremely bright people, yet they seemed resigned to their fates, and worse, resigned to imposing this "Death by Deck" on their various audiences.

Let me make it clear that the medium of PowerPoint isn't to be blamed here. Nor is its younger, smarter sibling, Keynote. When used creatively, it can be brilliant. When used the way most business people do today, it's lethal.

People seem to believe that they need to fill each and every screen, or slide, with as much type as possible. With charts and graphs. Statistics, facts, and figures. You'd think that they had bought the space at a very high price and needed to use it as efficiently as possible. Which, in a way, is true, but they were using it as inefficiently as possible.

Not only were there way—and I mean *way*—too many words on each slide, but the presenters all felt that it was their job to read each and every one of these words to their audience.

They had so much information they had to communicate that it had to all be packed onto the screen. What about the old rule about outdoor advertising—a maximum of eight words on a billboard? They hadn't heard about that—apparently it is an old rule, and these folks were specialists in a particular area. The principal reason that this horrible state of affairs has come to be is—The Deck.

The Deck—to paraphrase an old Saturday Night Live skit—it's a floor wax, *and* a dessert topping.

People produce The Deck, which is meant to be the official document regarding the particular issue at hand.

The problem is that while it may be a fairly comprehensive document explaining the problem and the author's solution to same, *it is not a presentation.* It is a recitation of (seemingly) every fact the agency can think of regarding the subject.

There is no story. No drama. No entertainment. No life. It just sits there on the desk or on the computer. When it is projected onto the screen it will induce narcolepsy among the most alert viewers in the room.

I have countless examples of stripping decks down to a reasonable number of words resulting in a compelling presentation. People doubt that it can be done, but it really isn't terribly difficult to do, and they are amazed at the different reaction they receive when they make the screen's message simple.

Simplicity is what we seek. In the visual as well as the oral expression of our ideas. Maybe more illuminating, and shocking to many people, is this: oftentimes, they don't even need the screen. *They* are far more interesting and compelling than the words on the screen will ever be.

My workshop participants never cease to be amazed by this, but they see it to be true every single time.

How can this be?

Because you are the message.

You are the star. Or at least you should be. I want you to be what the audience remembers. I want you to be persuasive and powerful. I want you to impress your audience with your command of your material and your skill in presenting it. Because I want them to trust you. Without trust, you will never sell any work of any real worth or importance. Trust is critical to every business relationship, and one of the most effective means of building trust is via presentation. In the beginning, when you don't know one another so well, the presentation is the principal way your client will get to know you. It's from this successful interaction that the client decides, "I like her. I'd like to hang out with her." And the relationship builds.

The words on the screen are usually a distraction to the audience. If you're reading the words, by the time you've gotten around to mouthing the words, the audience has finished reading them and is getting bored by hearing you say them.

Research conducted by a group at the University of New South Wales has confirmed that there is a scientific reason that your eyes glaze over as the speaker reads the bullet points on the screen. It is more difficult to process information if it is coming at you in the written and spoken form at the same time.

John Sweller, from the university's faculty of education, developed the "cognitive load theory."

"The use of the PowerPoint presentation has been a disaster," Professor Sweller said. "It should be ditched."

"It is effective to speak to a diagram, because it presents information in a different form. But it is not effective to speak the same words that are written, because it is putting too much load on the mind and decreases your ability to understand what is being presented."[1]

Amen. Thank you, Professor Sweller.

We all knew this, we just didn't have empirical proof.

There was a time when the various forms of visual support were called visual "aids." Today, most PowerPoint shows are like throwing an anchor to a drowning man.

Once, after I had railed against the evils of PowerPoint for most of the previous day, a workshop participant got up in front of the room and proceeded to read, word for word, what was on the screen. While looking directly at the screen the entire time.

Her colleagues stared at her uncomfortably.

I was beside myself, and remembered the words of the woman who had booked me for the engagement, "You've gotta be tough on them."

And so I was.

When the woman was through reading to us, I suggested that the same presentation could have been given as effectively by a cab driver who I could have recruited off the street. No knowledge of the topic or particular skill other than the ability to read English was required to duplicate her performance.

She wasn't happy, but she got the idea.

One of her colleagues said to me, "That was mean. Mean, but awesome."

THE ESTIMABLE JON STEEL, former head of planning at Goodby, Silverstein & Partners, and author of *Truth, Lies & Advertising,* as well as *Perfect Pitch,* is one of the all-time great presenters.

As a favor, he spoke to one of my classes. I asked him to give a PowerPoint presentation that he and his partners had actually used. He chose a new business presentation, which was over one and a half hours in length. It consisted of six slides. That's all. Five of the slides had one word on them. One of the slides had many words and numbers. It was a compilation of statistics that the client wanted to see. Jon did an hour and half with that as his visual arsenal.

Needless to say, he was brilliant. Each of those one-word slides triggered a wonderful piece of information or insight that allowed Jon to logically build an airtight argument for his point of view. Often, Jon never actually said the word that was on the screen. It appeared and remained there, underscoring everything he was saying, or in some cases, actually being the point of what he was saying. But always, the slides advanced the story that Jon was telling. Jon understands better than just about anybody that the best story wins. It doesn't even have to be the "right" story. It doesn't have to have all the answers. It doesn't even have to be factually correct. (There are about a thousand examples of this.) It just has to be the best story. The story that is most enjoyable to hear. The story that entertains. The story that allows you to show just how passionate you are about the subject. And maybe most importantly, the story that you believe.

This last point is critical.

Dick Sittig, the brilliant creative leader of Secret Weapon Marketing, once answered my question about the characteristics of a great presentation by saying, "Tell the truth."

I loved that then, and I still do.

Tell the truth. Your truth. Don't tell the audience anything that you don't believe.

At this point, most people in advertising are rolling their eyes and saying, "But we work in advertising."

And that's part of the reason most people in advertising give such lousy presentations.

They talk about what they think the client wants to hear or what their group came up with, but it's seldom what they personally, passionately believe.

Which is why the presentations are so gray and lifeless.

They approach the problem in the conventional way. Crank up the deck. Fill it with everything we know about the subject and project it on the screen while we take turns reading it.

And that's one of the reasons why most presentations, all over the world, suck.

In an Executive Education program at the Brandcenter, I asked the group of agency account managers in the session the following question: "What's the first thing you do after you've been given the assignment?" (This pertains to new business as well as to an existing client presentation.) One woman answered, "Get started on the deck."

"Really?"

I was floored. I suggested that they might want to figure out what they were going to do first. And maybe then actually sit down and figure out the answer to the assignment. After which, they could decide on the best way to deliver that answer. If it was to be a deck, so be it. But it's the last thing you do, not the first.

Several of the people in the session found this to be revolutionary thinking.

And that's another reason why most presentations, all over the world, suck.

Whenever you have a choice between complex and simple—choose simple. In the way you demonstrate your idea as well as the way you explain it. One of the most significant campaigns in the digital era was presented on paper boards.

*When we first presented BMW Films we were nervous. David Carter, who was as much the project's original author as anyone, had created these big wonderful boards that laid everything out in a very graphic way. It was a presentation device we had used often before: Circles and lines that showed how all the pieces fit together. But David did a masterful job with these. The whole idea was a bit convoluted to explain (remember, no one had ever done anything like it before.) But the boards made it all seem so simple and logical. It took us 30 minutes to present it, and 30 seconds for them to say yes. Never underestimate the power of simple, clear visual aids. God, I wish we had saved those boards.*

—Bruce Bildsten, executive creative director, Fallon

Keep it simple.

Never underestimate the power of simple, clear visual aids.

## HOW TO DO IT

Let me be really clear about this. I am not suggesting that you leave anything truly important out of your deck. I am suggesting that you should decide what is *truly important* about the material you've assembled and include *only that* in your deck. In fact, I'm suggesting that you must ascertain the most concise way to communicate that message and that the most concise way may be for you to talk about the truly important material while information that *supports* your argument is on the screen. That information may be words, or it may be visuals or a combination of the two. Simplify, simplify, simplify.

As I said, this isn't terribly difficult to do, but it does require us to spend the time necessary to determine what is critical to our argument, rather than putting everything we know about the subject up on the screen. Please understand—you've still got to pull together all the facts and data necessary to craft your argument, you just don't have to show all of them. Many people seem to think that if we show the client everything we did, they will see how much work we've done and, therefore, like us. No, they won't. Unless the purpose of the presentation is to literally show the client how much work we've done. It seldom is.

When we don't take the time to edit the information, we are abdicating what I believe is one of our most important responsibilities as an agency—using our experience, intellect, and talent to decide what's important and what isn't. In other words, having a point of view.

They want an answer to their business problem.

As I said, we've got to do all that work, assemble all that data and consider it carefully before deciding what to put into the deck and, therefore, into the presentation. All of that data doesn't belong in the presentation—it belongs in the leave-behind.

Here's what we need to do. Assemble all the data, information, facts, figures, and anything else you need to explain and justify your argument.

Write it up as a leave-behind. Then go through that document and create a deck that simply, clearly, and—dare I say?—elegantly presents your argument. In order to do that, you need to decide what each slide in the deck will look like. Is it words, visuals, or, as I suggested earlier, a combination of the two? Some of the smarter agencies I know get an art director involved at this point to make sure that the slides are uniformly appealing and consistent with our overarching message. Whatever you do, don't use clip art. It's boring. And go easy on the animation. Better to stick to some dissolves and/or cuts and forget about the flaming flip transition. Just because you can do it doesn't mean you should.

And then, you've got to sit down and write what I call the "Voice Over" for each slide. You've got to decide exactly what you will be saying as your audience is seeing the slide on the screen. Your words and the slides should be in perfect harmony—one supporting the other. Never put a slide on the screen before you are ready for the audience to see it. If the slide has type on it, they will read it. And they will stop paying attention to you while they're doing that. They can read faster than you can speak, so there will be yet another disconnection between you and the audience.

Remember, this is about making a human connection. And as Professor Sweller told us earlier, people have less chance of understanding your point if they are reading the same words you're saying.

People often complain that yes, this sounds great and makes sense, but it's more work, isn't it? Yes, it is more work. But aren't you willing to work a little harder to succeed more often and provide more value to your client?

Aren't you willing to work a little harder to sell your work and get what you want?

And ultimately, what happens is that it becomes easier and more efficient to do it this way because the meetings get shorter (you're giving them the Gift of Time) and you spend the time talking about what's truly important.

In chapter 1, we introduced the concept of doing an ad for our ads.

That's what the deck and ultimately the presentation should be. Use some of the creativity and story-telling ability that went into creating the work (regardless of what it is—creative, strategy, media recommendations, marketing initiatives, etc.) into *selling* the work. That's what the presentation is really all about and the deck is only there in service of that purpose.

If you follow this method, you will differentiate your firm from most of the other organizations in the world, you'll have shorter, more effective meetings, you'll sell more work, and you'll win more business. How does that sound?

## BEFORE AND AFTER

Take a look at the slides on the following pages. There are six pairs of slides. The slide on the left in each pair is a representation of what teams typically present on a daily basis around the world. The slide on the right of each pair is the result of a VCU Brandcenter team determining the most powerful, simple, and yet elegant way to support the speaker presenting that material.

Cindy Gallop, the founder and CEO of IfWeRanTheWorld. com assigned the teams the task of helping the beleaguered city of Braddock, Pennsylvania. Braddock had been a thriving community, but times, and the economy had passed Braddock by. The city was now in a well publicized battle for survival. An earlier co-operative venture with Levi's had produced some buzz, but little in the way of results. Cindy's assignment was to develop a corporate partnership with an appropriate firm and use the power of IfWeRanTheWorld.com to leverage the partnership.

In comparing the Before and After slides, I should point out that as bad as the Before slides are, I've seen far worse. I'm sure you have, too. None of the Before slides looks like a projection of a page of the New York City phone book, for instance. There is at least an attempt to minimize the number of bullet points on each slide, but why use bullet points when we're telling an emotional story?

*Before*

*After*

*The slide on the left, above, is typical of the evils perpetrated by people misusing PowerPoint. Not only is it ugly and boring, it's up there while the presenter is trying to begin her presentation in an interesting, engaging way. But the audience is reading the slide rather than connecting with the presenter. Far better to use a black slide as your first slide (above right). That way the audience is focused on you and not on some distracting information that isn't interesting in the first place.*

*Before*

*After*

*"Finding the Opportunity" is the sort of cliché we see regularly. It's in a different font than that used on the previous slide, probably because it was taken from another show or document. The timeline is hard to understand and confusing. The slide on the right is visually appealing and serves to support the presenter as he takes his audience through his story, with the presenter, not the screen, as the star.*

*Before*

*After*

*Yet another font (above left) and a chart that is as incomprehensible as it is complicated. The point of the slide is to identify the audience for craft beers. The slide on the right shows the audience and allows the presenter to explain who these people are. The visual is far more powerful than any chart.*

*Before*

Rolling Rock

Carve out a genuine space in the
thriving subsegment of the industry,
craft beer, while reinforcing Rolling
rocks unique positioning and quite
voice.

*After*

What is a "genuine" space? Another font is introduced and we feature
two typos. Did you find them? The slide on the right is a wonderful
encapsulation of the idea of a craft brewery in the American landscape.
Remember, we're trying to make an emotional connection. The slide
on the right does that.

*Before*

CREATIVE

- Print
- Outdoor
- PR
- Packaging

*After*

Once again, bullet points and a "table of contents" approach, rendered
in yet another font. I don't need a listing of the work I'm going to see.
I want to see the work. It's far more exciting and persuasive. This slide
would ideally be preceded by a black slide, allowing the presenter to
"frame" the work.

*Before*

*After*

**Summary**

- Rolling Rock and Braddock are a perfect marriage
- Leverage "small town" brand image
- Establish micro-brewery
- Incorporate "If We Ran the World" platform
- THANK YOU!

*Audiences crave endings. Give them one. Not a boring bullet-point list of what they just saw. ("Thank You!" is a crutch and the exclamation point is unforgivable.) The slide on the right is representative of the closing video, evoking patriotic feelings for the virtues of small town life, while summing up everything this team presented. The video was beautifully produced, with a powerful emotional voice over that was taken directly from copy found on the Rolling Rock website. When it ended, people in the audience were crying.*

As the screen went to black, Cindy Gallop, president and founder of IfWeRanTheWorld and former CEO of the advertising firm BBH New York, stood up and said just one word, "Wow." I probably don't have to point out that Cindy has seen her share of presentations. She then proceeded to talk about how this one was so brilliant because it was dramatic, powerful, and elegantly simple.

The next time you're putting together a presentation, sit down with the entire team and figure out what it is that you're trying to say. What's the big idea you want to leave with the audience? Then build your show from that idea backwards to the beginning. If we want to leave the audience with the idea that Rolling Rock is the perfect partner, every slide that leads up to that conclusion has to be consistent with that idea. Never, ever lose sight of the big idea that you're trying to communicate. It will help you make the right decisions every time and will ultimately lead you where you want to go.

## BE CAREFUL WHAT YOU WISH FOR

It is important to always know what we want to achieve in a presentation. It's not enough to just want to win, to get our way. We should have more on our minds than that. We should be there to win a piece of business by convincing the prospect that our answer will solve their problem and lead to economic success for their organization. Or we should be there to convince an existing client that the work we've prepared for them will not only be effective in the marketplace, it will enhance their brand's reputation over the long term. We want to become the very best presenters we can be—but we want to use this talent to serve our clients and our organizations. We should only be presenting work that we will be proud of. I've seen great presenters sell lousy work. In the long run, no one wins.

My colleague, Mark Fenske, founder of The Bomb Factory and legendary creative talent makes the point in this story:

*There is one outcome in making a presentation that almost no one thinks is a possible danger. And that is: You might get what you're after.*

*Winning sounds good, but it can be the worst outcome possible if you're not prepared for it. This is how I know: There was a time when I was not ready with new work when it was time to present to a client. I had the beginnings of an idea but I hadn't nailed it down.*

*Suddenly, the phone rang. The client was in the conference room.*

*I took out a yellow pad and put my rough thinking into as polished a finished product as five minutes allows.*

*To my compromised judgment it looked great. So I went into the meeting and presented the work I had just written.*

*The client bought it. At once, with hurrahs.*

*Everyone agreed it answered their problem. We all thought we were on the right track.*

*The meeting ended with smiles. Sounds like a success, doesn't it?*

*Meeting over, clients happy, where's the problem, eh?*

*Here: The ad sucked.*

*It had the outward appearance of lovely work but none of the inner structure.*

*It was glib instead of showing intelligence. It promised, it didn't prove.*

*It wasn't true enough or bold enough, it wasn't anything enough.*

*I had fallen into the trap of meeting the deadline but not meeting the standards of greatness. I solved the meeting, not the problem.*

*So we ended up producing a piece of work we all could tell was a turkey.*

*We were lucky, in that the ad was small and ran in a magazine no one read.*

*But it easily could have mattered. Don't be fooled.*

*A good meeting is not the goal.*

*Great work is. Eyes on the prize.*

—**Mark Fenske, professor, VCU Brandcenter**

# EIGHT

# ORGANIZING THE PRESENTATION

Well, if the deck isn't the first thing we do, how do we organize our thinking into a powerful presentation? Fair question.

What I suggest you do is yet more work. Sorry, but if you want to be good at something, you have to work at it.

At this point you and your teammates should have decided what the presentation is supposed to accomplish (believe me, that is never simple), and you're ready to begin. But **do not begin to organize the presentation until you have unanimous agreement on what you're trying to accomplish and how you'll do it.** So figure that out first.

Then, sit down and write the presentation. Or your part of it. I think it's good if the presentation speaks with one voice, so it may be best for one person to write the whole thing, if possible. This does not mean that you are writing the words that you and your teammates will speak. Rather, it means that you are formulating the argument, complete with support points that will be necessary to make your case for your ideas.

One excellent way to wrestle the presentation to the ground is to lay it out on a series of Post-it notes, in the manner of a storyboard. You can put them all down in front of you or stick them on a board and move them around until you've got them in the order that brings the show to life.

In working with my students on specific presentations, we always get into a room with a whiteboard and some markers. We draw frames on the wall that represent each individual point we're trying to make. It's like the Post-it notes, but on the whiteboard. It's very helpful to the students to see the different components of the presentation laid out before them. Many have said that it helps them focus their thinking. Whatever works is what I believe in using.

Ideally, each of these frames representing one idea builds on the last frame and foreshadows the next frame. When you get good at this, every single frame (or slide in the finished show) will lead directly and logically to the next, taking your audience by the hand and walking them through your story to the end—where you get what you want and they are happy to give it to you.

When crafting each of these frames you should figure out what the segue is from one frame to the next. You don't have to create the actual language at this point, but you do want to think through how the first slide sets up the second, which leads into the third, and so forth. This way, you are ensuring that there will be a sustainable logical flow to your story. If the frames don't lead into one another, the audience will get lost. I think of these disconnects as bumps in the road, and too many bumps will cause your audience to fall off the truck. We want to build a smooth road with no bumps.

The next step is one that most people omit. Design the visuals. What does each slide look like? They might be words, or they might simply be visuals. Or, they might be both. Figure out what will help you and your team make your case most effectively. You might not use slides. However you decide to go, determine what visual support is consistent with the points you're trying to make, accurately reflects the material you're presenting, and amplifies what you're going to say.

This is where you might want to get an art director involved. If there's one on your team, great; if not, go find one in the agency. Show her the presentation as you have it laid out and explain the story you're going to tell and the conclusion you're going to reach. She can then create a "look" for the show that holds it all together and reinforces the ultimate point you're trying to make. When combined with your words, the look of the show will magnify the impact of your message. One and one should equal three.

And lastly, write the voice-over. These are the actual words you're going to say as you go through your visuals and tell your story to your audience.

This is different from Step One, writing the presentation. In Step One, you're laying out the ideas you want to present and their most effective order. In writing the voice-over, you're laying out the actual words that will communicate those ideas. But you're not necessarily writing a script. It's more like an outline. It's not necessary to repeat these words as first written. What is necessary is that you and your teammates are able to express the *ideas* these words represent rather than each and every word as written. Many people will lay out a series of "marks" they want to hit, or points that need to be made, and let the actual language fill itself in around each of those points. That's why I don't recommend that the author of the presentation insist that each person in the show deliver the lines as written. One complaint that many people in agencies have voiced to me is that they are told to read lines *verbatim* and not to deviate from the script as written, usually by the "boss." This is a mistake. The people on the team need to read the written words and make them their own. They need to find a way to express the written ideas in their own language and style. Only then will they be their authentic selves, which, as we've said, is what we're seeking. If forced to read someone else's language, it won't come off as their own thinking. It will come off as false. And that will be the end of any emotional connection with your audience.

Once the words are written, each individual needs to make them their own. They need to know the material. And they need to know everyone's part, not just theirs. Notice I didn't say memorize them. Don't. As I said earlier, memorizing will get you in big trouble. You will forget and you will then get completely derailed because rather than knowing the *ideas* you're trying to communicate, you know the *words*. So you'll be trying to remember the precise word you memorized, and when you don't come up with it quickly enough to satisfy yourself, you'll panic. I've seen it time and again. So don't memorize. The only exception would be when you are trying to communicate an important quote or a salient fact, such as a particular date that must be delivered accurately. You might consider having that quote on the screen in type rather than relying solely on your memory. Reading a quote off the screen is one of the very few times that it's acceptable to read the words that are on the screen. The other big problem with memorizing is that your presentation will *sound* like you memorized it. We've all seen that. It's like a bad actor in a movie. It isn't authentic, and your audience will dismiss what you're saying.

It's far better to speak from the heart, to search for your words, even make the occasional mistake, than it is to deliver a perfect, memorized speech.

Let's remember that this is about persuasion, and someone who appears to be regurgitating memorized material is not persuasive.

## THE ACTION FORMAT

My friend Sheila Campbell invented a format for planning presentations. It's an acronym, so it's cheesy, and this one is particularly cheesy, but it's smart and it will be very helpful if you use it.

Sheila calls it the ACTION Format, and here it is:

**A** is for Attention. Every good presentation begins with an attention-getting device of some kind. This can be something you say or show. It could be a video that starts the show before anyone has said anything. Or, if you're using a deck, the first slide might be an arresting image on the screen. It's why rock bands still have smoke bombs. Ideally, the first thing out of your mouth will be something interesting or compelling. Something other than "We're really excited to be here today." Say something that makes us want to listen to what follows. It should be a simple declarative sentence. It shouldn't be, "So, okay, so, here we are, um . . ." If you can just train your teammates and yourself to eliminate the "so" and all the other space-holder jargon from their speech, your presentation will be infinitely more powerful. Start clean and strong.

One day in a workshop, a senior-level planner told me that she had never tried to do that before, but that today she was going to begin with something that she hoped would be interesting, personal, and make everyone want to pay attention. She stood up in front of the room and said, "When I was twenty-four, I met a Spanish chef." I clapped immediately.

C is for Capsule. The capsule is two or three sentences that sum up the entire presentation. They should fit on an index card.

In *Perfect Pitch*, Jon Steele writes of a time when he was first working in the UK. His boss asked him to write a two-hour new business presentation. Jon wrote the presentation and gave it to his boss, who read every word. Then his boss handed him an index card and said, "Now write it on that."

This is a great way to get a handle on what it is that you really want to say. I frequently see student presentations that rush over important ideas to get to one that isn't really very important. It's critical that a presenter understands what she has to say that is truly important and that logically explains her position in such a way that it is impossible to misinterpret it. So write down the three big ideas. Your presentation should be so simple that you can boil it down to just a few sentences. And notice that I said *simple,* not *simplistic.* Please understand that this capsule won't necessarily *be* part of the show, but it *sums up* the entire show. Accordingly, you won't be able to write it until you've laid out the organization of the show, but it will serve as a decision-making guide during the writing of the show because you will know exactly where the show is going and what it's about, and you will be in a great position to eliminate any ideas that aren't consistent with the capsule.

T is for Theme. All good presentations have a theme that holds them together. You need to decide on the theme and then be sure that all of the ideas and thoughts you present are consistent with that or can somehow be brought back to the theme.

When the folks at Cramer-Krasselt are organizing and writing their presentations, they continually interrupt one another and ask the question "Is it on theme?" It may be a cool idea, but if it isn't on theme, it's out.

This is why theatrical productions begin with an overture. The musical themes you will hear in the show are introduced in the overture, then repeated throughout the show and then reprised once more at the end. What would any of the Indiana Jones films be like without the rousing John Williams theme that swells regularly throughout the movie? How about the menacing notes in *Jaws?*

A recent presentation to Sony was held together by the theme of "magic." Sony's own mission statement talks about their belief in the magic of technology, so the student team began their presentation by talking about magic and the role that it had played in the life of one of the presenters. She then went on to talk about Sony's belief in magic and the fact that the new product they were introducing just wasn't magical. But that if it were positioned differently, opposing different competition and offered to a different target audience, it could indeed be magical. In presenting the creative work, they said that in order to do it properly, a little magic would be required. They then showed an extremely clever stop-motion animated video that showcased the product in a magical light.

Are you getting the point? Simply practice this idea and your presentations will be instantly better.

I is for Information. This is the stuff you have to tell and show them. This is the data, the strategy, the business plan, the ideas, the work. Everything you need to have to convince them of the brilliance of your point of view.

O is for Open to Listen. Admittedly, this is a bit of a cheat, but it's important advice. During a presentation, you must always be listening with your eyes as well as your ears. You've got to be constantly aware of what's going on in the room. Is your client following your argument? Does he understand each point you're trying to make? Often, the only way you'll be able to know the answer to those questions is to watch the way he reacts. In certain situations, someone may say something at some point that is critical to your success. They may reveal something that you can use to bolster your argument. Or they may tell you that they're already on board and want you to move forward. If you don't pick up these cues, you will lose all credibility.

This happens more often than you might think. When my partners and I had just started our agency, we were invited to pitch our services to a local bank. This represented a great opportunity for a new agency, so we took it very seriously. At that time we hadn't yet figured out what roles we should be playing. We decided that Stanley, who had actually been an account executive on a bank account at Doyle Dane Bernbach, and who was further qualified by owning a suit, should serve as the principal presenter in the pitch.

Stanley was seated to my left with our third partner, John, to his left. The people who held at least a portion of our fate in their hands, Lee Mumford and Steve Garnett, sat directly across the table from us.

Stanley was cruising along, recounting all of his experience and the wonderful creative thinking we would bring to the account, when Lee, who was the director of marketing said, "I'm convinced. You've got the business."

Needless to say, I was really excited by this, but unfortunately, Stanley didn't hear Lee. So he just kept going. It wasn't as if Lee had whispered his comment. He said it at a perfectly audible level. But Stanley, God bless him, was so into what *he* was saying that he never heard Lee. So he kept going. To my horror and Lee's chagrin. Lee let him go on for a while, and then said to me, "Peter, if you don't shut him up, I'm going to take the account back."

That was all I needed to hear. I immediately placed my left hand over Stanley's mouth. He did a spit take and was shocked. "What!?" he shouted.

"We won, Stan, we got the account and now it's time to leave."

Everyone had a bit of a chuckle and we agreed to leave and get back to them the following day.

This story is true and it's only one, admittedly dramatic, example of what can happen when we're not Open to Listen.

But believe me, the same thing happens every day in one form or another all over the world. Don't let it happen to you.

**N** is for Next Steps. This is what you want to accomplish as a result of the presentation. We must ask ourselves, "Why are we doing this? What do we really want them to say or think or do?" You and your teammates must come to an agreement on a simple, clear statement of purpose for the presentation. This may strike you as obvious, but I assure you that based on the number of presentations I've seen over the years that do not have any clear point, it is not.

Now what we just went through is not the order in which I would complete these steps. It just happens to be the order of the letters that spell ACTION.

The order isn't all that important except for the beginning. Start with Next Steps. Before you do anything, establish what it is that you want out of the presentation. And not just something as easy as "We want them to buy our campaign." That isn't specific enough. I want you to agree not just on the idea that they will buy the campaign, but *why* they will buy the campaign. Make it specific and clear so that it leaves no room for equivocation or doubt. That may take a good deal of discussion with your colleagues, or it may not, but it must be done. How can we determine how to get somewhere if we don't know where we're going? And remember, we're discussing how to *organize* the presentation, not the order in which we will *deliver* the presentation.

This first step is critical for several reasons, paramount among them the rule that nothing will be included in the presentation that isn't on point. We start with what we want and work backwards to the beginning. Then, when we're building the presentation, we must be diligent in determining if each element leads us to precisely what we want, or if it has been included because it's cool or we like what it says about us, or it gives our teammate Marlon a chance to show off, or any of a thousand bad reasons for its inclusion.

This is why we won't have Marlon play "Layla" on his electric guitar. The seven-minute version with the birds tweeting at the end. Yes, it's still a cool song, and he plays it really well, but it has nothing to do with what we want out of the presentation.

Okay, it's a metaphor. And you may think I'm exaggerating. I am, but only a little bit to make my point. Time and again I see agencies and individuals present elements and ideas that have nothing to do with why we were all there. The purpose of one or more of their elements was incomprehensible. But they did it because they could. Or, maybe more frequently, they fell in love with their idea. We all fall in love with our own ideas. The trick is to know when to fall out of love with these ideas and get out of the presentation.

Sometimes "Layla" slips into presentations as a way to take up time. Many agencies believe that if they're given two hours, they should use two hours, regardless of whether or not their ideas require that amount of time to be compellingly presented. Only use as much time as you need to present your thinking. No more, no less. Give them back half an hour and they will love you for it. Almost all presentations are too long anyway. So figure out what you want and exclude anything that doesn't get you there, no matter how brilliant or cool it might be. Remember the concept of ruthless exclusion.

Then you are free to proceed. A likely scenario could be that once you've agreed on what you want, the Next Steps, you then begin to assemble all of the Information you will need to make your argument. Then, you establish a Theme that will hold it all together and create an Attention-getting device. By the way, this device may very well foreshadow the ultimate purpose of the presentation. Toward the end of the process, you should be able to write the Capsule, and you must always be Open to Listen.

So there it is. The ACTION format for *organizing* presentations, not *delivering* presentations. It works. Thank Sheila Campbell. And while we're thanking Sheila, we should also thank Anne Bologna for her explanation of how she puts her presentations together.

*In preparing for a presentation the first step is to figure out the main points I want to get across, but that's only the beginning. The next step is figuring out how to bring those points to life in the most compelling and interesting way possible. For example, I may show a provocative image and talk from that for the entire presentation. Or, I might use a handful of head-snapping "fun facts" to shake up an audience's perceptions. On rare occasions where no audio or visual aids were available, my presentations were usually best because I was forced to internalize my point of view and express it in a completely personal, human way—which is the essence of good storytelling. Regardless of having access to visual aids, I always try and make a presentation personal as much as possible. I might share an experience about a client's product or service. Or I may tell a self-deprecating story about something related to the topic. Humor isn't right for every occasion, but more often than not it tends to make my message (and myself) more, not less, credible. It also happens that humor is in character for me, so I use it whenever I can. I'm also a big believer in the rule, "Tell 'em what you're going to tell 'em, tell 'em, and then tell 'em what you told 'em." I'm obsessed with clarity. There's nothing worse than listening to an interesting speaker and walking away wondering, "What was the point, again?" Last and not least, I always try to finish earlier than expected. It's a pleasant surprise for the audience and the Q & A part is generally the most satisfying for the listeners.*

**—Anne Bologna, general manager, Cramer-Krasselt**

# NINE

---

# REHEARSE, REHEARSE, REHEARSE

N o one idea, tip, or technique will cure as many ills as knowing your material. And the only way to do that is to rehearse. You may see a contradiction in that statement. Namely, that you know the material so well you don't have to rehearse. Well, that's just wrong. We're talking about two things here—being familiar with the material you're planning on presenting, and knowing the story you're going to tell in order to convince your audience that your material is the answer to their problem.

You must first make yourself completely familiar with the material, and then you must develop and learn the story you're going to use to sell it. We talked about the dangers of memorization in earlier chapters, but based upon what I see in my workshops, it bears repeating. Memorization will get you in trouble. You will be in front of the room trying to remember the exact words that you memorized, eventually you will fail, and then you will be stuck. Because you're not familiar with the *ideas* of the presentation, you only learned the *exact words*.

Another problem with memorization: your delivery will sound memorized. Remember, we're telling a story here. We're painting a word picture for our listeners. It should seem as if we're thinking of these words for the first time as we say them. In fact, it should feel as if we're telling this particular story for the first time. It should not sound like a regurgitation of facts you memorized.

When we see a bad actor in a movie, it sounds as if he's repeating the lines he learned. When we see a good actor, it sounds as if she's saying words that just popped into her head.

Big difference.

Particularly because we're striving for authenticity.

Since most of the presentations that ad agencies give are team presentations, it's critical that the team rehearse together. But as I travel around the country working with agencies, the people who give these presentations tell me that they rarely rehearse together for anything but new business, and even then not all the time. The chief marketing officer of a large international agency told me that he couldn't get the top management members of a team working on a very big pitch to rehearse at all. They lost to an agency that I know had been rehearsing their pitch for a week.

Not rehearsing isn't just setting yourself up for failure, it's idiotic.

This is appalling to me, and yet another reason why so many presentations are just terrible.

It's not enough to let the individuals on the team go off on their own and prepare their own parts. Yes, they should do that, but the team needs to come together to craft the final presentation together. And not just in new business. It may not be as sexy, but agencies need to realize that virtually all presentations are new business presentations. Even existing clients are evaluating the purchase decision they've made, no matter how long ago. Many of these clients have other brands or other budgets that could be awarded to your agency without even going through a pitch. If they are consistently impressed with your presentations, there's a good chance that you could gain some new business organically. And don't think for a minute that your competitors aren't actively courting all of your existing clients. I assure you that they are.

Another reason for rehearsing presentations to existing clients—clients want to feel that you care. Not just about your work, but about the relationship. Presenting a smooth, entertaining, thoughtful discussion of your work is, in a way, a compliment to your client. Just as in a personal relationship, you cannot take the other party for granted.

If we want to sell our very best work to our clients, we need to be persuasive and in order to be persuasive; we need to craft our argument skillfully. That is accomplished through rehearsal.

Never let one of your teammates off the hook with regard to team rehearsal. Even if his name is on the building. Everyone must hear everyone else speak. Each member of the team needs to know what the other is going to say because in the heat of battle, it's likely that someone will leave something important out, and you'll be there to pick up the ball and make that critical point.

Likewise, you can't let the "old pro" in the group off the hook either. Okay, he's done a thousand of these presentations. I don't care. I want him in there practicing with the team.

Also, by rehearsing together, you will make the presentation better. You've got four or five smart people in a room listening to everything and critiquing as they go. That's how it gets better.

So appoint someone to be in charge of scheduling all the presentation meetings, including the rehearsals. She doesn't have to be the senior person on the team, but she has to have ultimate authority to call meetings and expect people to show up. Everyone on the team must acknowledge her as The Pitch Ayatollah, and abide by her schedule. If people can't make the meetings, they're out of the pitch. If they don't come to rehearsal, they won't be in the pitch.

If you establish some of these basic rules in your organization, your presentations will get better immediately. It will probably require changing not just the way you do things, but some cultural changes as well. Which is fine. Just lay down the law and stick to it.

By rehearsing together, you'll not only know each others' parts and ultimately make the presentation better, you'll build a real sense of teamwork, of the kind of camaraderie that clients love and are instinctively drawn to.

> *Often the failures in this business were not about content as much as they were about style—particularly how well the team interacted within itself. The issue is not merely chemistry with an audience, but since we always present as a group, it is equally about chemistry between the presenters. Clients sense team. If it's stilted or not interactive in a genuine, relaxed way, chances are greatly reduced. If it is clicking, it's infectious, and likability can at least diminish some content shortcomings if there are any. When we are clicking, we have almost always won—of course, good work and thinking have to be above average to begin with.*
>
> *What I think is often forgotten in presentations is that they are not solo performances—they are troupe performances.*
>
> **—Peter Krivkovich, president,**
> **chief executive officer, Cramer-Krasselt**

People in the business spend a lot of time creating their work. And then almost no time figuring out how to present it. Agency creatives tell me that they talk about what they're going to say and do in the cab on the way to the meeting.

This is ridiculous. They're not giving their work a chance. Their work, that expression of themselves that they have slaved over day and night, is slid across the table and right into what I call a "jump ball." It could go either way, and the decision is out of the agency's hands. Great work deserves a chance to live. The way to ensure that is to rehearse the way in which you sell it.

An important step in organizing the presentation is deciding who should be on the team. Your first thoughts on this subject may change during rehearsal when the group has the opportunity to hear one another deliver their parts and observe the chemistry or lack thereof in the room. You may also discover that while the people you've chosen for the team are the logical choices, they may not be the right choices to build the emotional connection we're seeking.

*During the course of a project I hold several "casting sessions." The first is designed to get the right minds working against the problem so that we end up with the most creative, surprising, and effective ideas. The second casting session gets us to who will present those ideas to the client, because the team who came up with them may very well not be the right one to sell them and get them produced. Some creative teams don't like that, thinking they should represent their own work. To them I always say, "What will make you more proud at the end of the day: the chance to hear yourself talk for an hour or the chance to hear yourself talked about for years?*

—**Darren Moran, executive creative director, DraftFCB**

We talked earlier about the need to create an "ad for your ads." Just spend a bit of time bringing the same level of creativity to *selling* the work as you brought to *creating* the work. That doesn't seem like too much to ask, does it?

In order to do that, you've got to rehearse. I've had people at agencies tell me that they don't like to rehearse because they don't want to "lose my spontaneity." To which I say, "horseshit."

The appearance of spontaneity is the product of rehearsal.

The best presenters in the business rehearse as much as they can. Steve Jobs spends a minimum of three weeks rehearsing his MacWorld addresses. Bruce Springsteen and the E Street Band spend hours rehearsing segues between songs that they've been playing for 30 years.

Let me quote from Carmine Gallo's book, *The Presentation Secrets of Steve Jobs:*

> Steve Jobs spends hours rehearsing every facet of his presentation. Every slide is written like a piece of poetry, every presentation staged like a theatrical experience. Yes, Steve Jobs makes a presentation look effortless but that polish comes after hours and hours of grueling practice. Steve Jobs has improved his style over time. If you watch video clips of Steve Jobs' presentations going back twenty years (available on YouTube) you will see that he improves significantly with every decade. The Steve Jobs of 1984 had a lot of charisma but the Steve Jobs of 1997 was

a far more polished speaker. The Steve Jobs who introduced the iPhone in 2007 was even better. Nobody is born knowing how to deliver a great PowerPoint presentation. Expert speakers hone that skill with practice.[1]

Rehearse, rehearse, rehearse and then rehearse some more.

And, if possible, rehearse in the room in which you'll be giving the presentation. Feel the space; get an idea for what it'll be like with people filling it. Rehearse where everyone will sit. Use everything in the room to your advantage. If you don't like the way the furniture is arranged, change it. Just put it back the way it was before you leave. If too much light comes shining through the windows to suit you and your visuals, put up some temporary drapes. Do whatever it is that will contribute to the success of your presentation. One of your objectives is to be memorable, so don't be afraid to change the room to suit your purposes and add drama to your story. Remember Jeff Goodby's Sega story?

And rehearse with the actual projection equipment that will be used in the presentation.

This may seem like an unimportant detail, but as Pam Scott explains, failure to do so can be a devastating mistake.

*Once I was asked to give the keynote address to an auditorium of about 3,000 creative types. The day before my speech, I went for an AV check put on by the conference. By the time I arrived, the AV team was so worn out they were adamant about not hooking up my computer for a run-through of my slides. They insisted that they knew exactly how to make my slides work. "No worries," they said. Because my presentation was hugely reliant on visuals, I pushed back. We bickered for about 20 minutes, less than the time it would have taken to do the visual check, until I finally relented.*

*The next day I showed up for my speech. I was the second of two keynote speakers. The first guy was killing the audience. About five minutes into his speech, I heard someone scream "We love you, man!" from the audience. Then other people started offering other enthusiastic cheers. The applause throughout his speech was nearly deafening but it was especially so during his standing ovation. He left the stage pumped up like Mick Jagger. Who wouldn't have? Then it was my turn.*

*I hopped up on stage full of as much positive energy as I can muster (which is a pretty darned healthy amount) and looked behind me and saw nothing. No slides. I made a few comments about the previous speaker, turned around and, still, nothing. My positive energy started to turn to anxiety as I tried to wing it without my slides. Sweat started to bead up on my face and was beginning to drip from my hands. Five minutes later (still no slides) all the crazed energy the last speaker had generated was almost completely dead. I had killed the room in the exact opposite manner.*

*Finally, after about 8–10 minutes, my slides magically appeared. I found my footing and made it through the speech. Not my best performance, but it ended better than it started. What I found out later was that my then-boyfriend Tim had jumped onstage to fix the problem. The know-it-all AV folks actually didn't know so much after all! When I found this out, I knew I had met the man I was going to marry!*

**What I Learned**

*Even if you have to go nut-ball on a reluctant AV team, always insist on an AV check and set-up of your slides.*

*Never go on stage without seeing your slides projected first. Make the AV team (not you) sweat it out.*

*Marry someone with terrific AV skills so you always come packin'. ;-)*

—**Pam Scott, founder, The Curious Company**

## OWN IT

Once you have developed the presentation and are fully rehearsed, know the material backwards and forwards and are ready to go, you've got to do something else that most people never think about.

You've got to commit to it.

You've got to own it.

It's not just yours, it's you.

You may very well be part of a team that developed the presentation and you're actually presenting just a part of it.

But it is all yours. You are responsible.

You must be accountable.

You can't settle for knowing your part.

You've got to know everyone's part.

You have to take personal responsibility for the success or failure of the presentation. Not just whether or not you look good.

You've got to know the whole thing. Every idea. Every slide. Every segue. Someone will forget something. Someone may have an emergency at the last moment and not be able to be there. Even if everyone is there, you've got to know the whole thing.

And you have to commit to it.

You have to give it just the way you rehearsed it.

With heart and soul.

With Clarity, Conviction, and Grace.

You must stand and deliver.

This does not mean that you are not flexible and open to the reactions of the audience. You must be in complete harmony with the audience, sensing their level of understanding and comprehension. You must be able to make adjustments on the fly. If they're not getting something, you've got to make the point in a way that they do get before you move on to the next point. Because that's the way great presentations work—they are built step by step, point by point, until the argument that has been constructed is irrefutable.

It's easy to be comfortable and confident when things are going well, but a lot harder when they aren't. That's when your commitment will truly be tested.

Time and again in my advertising career I was in presentations that were clearly headed south for one reason or another. You must do everything you can to stop that slide to the south. Change gears, ask questions, shake up the meeting. But do something.

Sometimes, it just requires being calm. Things are seldom as bad as they seem, and if you just hang in there and project an air of cool and calmness, you'll probably be okay. Remember, the audience doesn't know what you and your team are supposed to be saying.

But other times, things *are* as bad as they seem.

### What Won Kim Said

*The most uncomfortable presentation I have ever been a part of was back in the early days at BSSP. We were called Butler, Shine & Stern back then. This was long before we had proved ourselves to the consultants, so of the many reviews we did, some were legit, but most were not. Daewoo came sniffing around in the mid-to-late 1990s, and a number of West Coast agencies, all about our size, ran to the trough. We were introduced to Won Kim, a young Korean/American who spoke flawless English, who was to be our main contact. We put together a pitch and I flew to L.A. with Stern and an account supervisor. Five minutes before show time, our account supervisor tells us that she isn't feeling well. But she seems to power through it like a pro, and we don't really think much more about it.*

*We walk into the room, and Won Kim greets us charismati-
cally. Behind him sit at least a dozen Korean men, in various
stages of seniority, and we notice almost immediately that most
do not have anywhere near the proficiency in the English language that Won Kim does.*

*Stern opens our meeting, and then the account supervisor
stands up to deliver her bit, and after a few short sentences, she
does a face plant onto the table. I don't remember much of a
commotion around this, and that might have been because Stern
and I were in her face, shaking her and trying to make certain
she wasn't dead. She wasn't, and we got her up into her seat,
where she stayed, clutching a water bottle for the duration of
the presentation.*

*The next memorable bit of that pitch, and the only other
thing I do recall beyond our not winning it, was presenting
the work to the room, and noticing midway through reading
my scripts that more than one of them were out as cold as our
account supervisor. I counted at least four of them doing that
"heads back, mouths open" brand of sleeping. But I didn't want
to be disrespectful, so I soldiered on without a word. When the
meeting was over, they all woke up and clapped enthusiastically.*

*After the pitch, Won Kim told us how amazing our presen-
tation was. He said that to a man, his associates all enjoyed the
meeting immensely.*

*I said, "Won Kim, they were out cold."*

*"Sleeping?" he said. "No, this is cultural, John, they were simply resting their eyes, but they heard every word."*

*"Won Kim, they were lights out in London, doing that Three Stooges 'e-bee-bee-bee' sleeping noise. I put the room into a coma," I said.*

*But he vehemently disagreed and assured me they were at rapt attention. We left believing that we had lost, and we had.*

**—John Butler, partner, creative director, BSSP**

If you're in the business for any length of time, you're going to find yourself in a meeting similar to John's. The thing to remember is that even if things seem to be heading south, you still might win if you stay committed and soldier on. My agency won a presentation once simply because we "showed grace under pressure," according to the client.

One thing I am sure of is this—if you give up, you won't win.

## GETTING STARTED

The hardest part of presenting for a lot of people is just getting going.

We see this all the time. People stumble and fumble their way into an opening. Which usually isn't much of an opening.

This is typical: "So, I'm going to talk to you today, about like, you know, how we kinda think we can sorta, you know!"

If I had a dollar for every presentation that begins with the word "so" there would be a New Big Three of wealthiest men in the country—Gates, Buffet, and Coughter.

I realize that "so" is a staple of the current lexicon, but it is amazing how much more interesting presentations are when they begin without the word "so."

Or the recently popular, "Okay, so."

Or any of the crutches that are sprinkled throughout discourse today.

That doesn't mean that we should all use it.

Let's call it the "so language."

This is a serious problem for young people. Perfectly intelligent, competent individuals with five or six years on the job and a couple of promotions under their belt are not juniors. Yet everywhere I go, I see people who fit this description but who come off as juniors because they speak in this strange dialect.

Whatever the reason, get rid of it, because if you speak "so," you will forever be labeled a junior.

I am often reluctant to point this out to the people in my workshops because I don't want them to think that I'm picking on them for something trivial. Yet I'm pleased to report that in almost every case (of hundreds every year) they embrace my comments and agree that it sounds terrible. When we sit together and watch a video recording of their presentations, this becomes vividly clear. Most people are appalled to discover that they speak "so." And they swear that they will work to rid themselves of what I think is just an affectation.

"So" is a perfectly good adverb and an even better conjunction. Use it in those ways. Just don't start your presentation with it.

Start clean. No "so's," "um's," "like's," etc.

I have had CEOs say, "I'm begging you. If you can just get them to stop saying 'sorta' and 'kinda' I will be eternally grateful."

There is another affront on spoken English abroad in the land. I call it the Attack of the Adverbs. "Actually," "basically" and "essentially" are now liberally sprinkled throughout the content of presenters every day. Usage of these words, often incorrectly by the way, has become an epidemic on the scale of Val Speak. I've seen a presenter use "actually" three times in one run on sentence. It doesn't necessarily make the speaker sound like a junior; it makes the speaker sound unintelligent (I thought that was a nicer word than "stupid").

And while we're at it, no "probably's" or "coulda's" or "shoulda's." I have seen several presentations in which the presenter, going into her big impassioned close—trying to sell us the work—actually said, "So, we think this work will probably accomplish what we want." "Probably." There's a powerful statement. A real ringing endorsement.

There is no room for "probably" in a presentation, or in any kind of persuasive argument, for that matter. The audience wants certainty, conviction, and confidence. They don't want "probably." They don't need a guarantee, but they want to be assured that you at least believe your recommendation will be successful. If you don't think so, why should they?

How *should* we begin?

By saying nothing.

That's right. When it is your turn to speak, simply look at the audience. Make eye contact with someone. Smile. And be silent for a few seconds. Everyone in the room will be staring at you. Which is exactly what we want. By being silent you are accomplishing several things. As we just said, you're getting their attention without really doing anything. You're providing some punctuation, which is necessary because we need to give the audience the idea that something new is about to begin. What just occurred is over. Now it's your turn.

And we are showing the audience that we are in charge of the room. We're comfortable with the situation and in our own skin. You might even walk around a little bit.

Because most people are terrified of silence, they tend to fill up all the available airtime with noise. That's what the audience is used to experiencing. When you give them something different, something fresh, they like it. And they are one big step closer to liking you, which is what we're after.

When the room is silent and you have everyone's attention—you should begin.

Begin with a simple declarative sentence. Preferably one that is interesting and/or provocative. Something that gets the audience's attention. "Good morning, it's great to be here," has probably been said a few times already. Even if you're the first presenter of the day, skip the "Good morning, it's great to be here," and **say something that makes the audience believe that it's great to be here. That you are going to be delivering one interesting, maybe even entertaining, presentation.**

As we said earlier, this is why rock bands still use smoke bombs.

Why movies now get right into it and save the credits for the end. Why things blow up as soon as possible in summer blockbusters. Why James Bond movies all start with some fantastic action set piece. Why the first sentence in a good novel is often powerful and therefore remembered for decades. If not longer.

Grab your audience's attention right at the beginning. And don't ever let it go.

Remember our "When I was 24, I met a Spanish chef" story? Start clean and strong.

I cannot overemphasize the importance of this point. The first sound out of your mouth is what the audience will remember. They will immediately formulate an opinion of you based on the first sound you make. (They've already got an opinion of you based upon the way you look, so this is your chance to confirm that or change it.)

It may be that your attention-getting opening isn't even something you say. You might want to open with a powerful image on the screen behind you. Or a stirring, provocative quote. Russell

Davies kids around with a musical fanfare to make the point that something important is about to happen. You get the idea. Get their attention.

When using images on a screen, no matter what the program, please remember this—nothing should be on the screen until it suits your purposes. Nothing should be there until the image is perfectly aligned with what you are saying and results in an important point being made.

Sometimes that point isn't even stated. It's the sum of the image on the screen and the words you are saying combining to produce yet a third, more significant concept. When this happens, things can be really exciting. You are like a medieval wizard creating some powerful alchemy out of words and images to produce magic.

Failing that, and most of us will, keep it simple. Maybe the magic should come later.

Start with a black screen. Let the first slide fade up at precisely the moment it is aligned with your idea, producing the result you are seeking.

And don't be afraid to go back to black (or white, if you choose) after you've made your point. If what's on the screen isn't in alignment with the point you're trying to make, let it fade away. This is another form of punctuation and one that the audience will understand completely.

How many presentations have you seen that begin with a slide up on the screen stating the title of the presentation, the subtitle of the presentation, the logos of the organizations involved in the lower left and right corner, and right in the middle of the two (or more) logos—today's date?

That slide sits there while the speaker fumbles along, sliding into a beginning using the word "so." I've seen literally thousands of presentations like this.

You know, having the date up there on the screen is so helpful to everyone in attendance, I've often suggested to presenters that they put a real-time running digital clock in the corner of the screen so that everyone in the audience will know exactly what time it is as well as the date. It might also give them an indication of whether or not they have any chance of making it to the end.

Start strong and clean.

Remember—Clarity, Conviction, and Grace. Starting Strong and Clean is the way to begin.

## THE LITTLE VOICE

Does this ever happen to you? You're presenting your material, but you're having trouble focusing on *what* you're saying and doing because you can't seem to stop thinking about *how* you're doing. You're convinced that the audience doesn't understand a word you're saying. You think your hair is a mess, or your glasses make you look dorky, or any one of a thousand other things that aren't going to be of any help to you.

If so, take heart, you're not alone. A very high percentage of the people I work with suffer from what I call "the little voice." Little Julio (or Little Marie, or Little Kate) is up in our heads offering all kinds of not very helpful commentary. "This isn't going well," "They hate your ideas," "Go faster and get this over with." We've got to quiet Little Julio down. Eventually we need to tell him to go wait in the car. The trick is to concentrate. Commit and concentrate. You've rehearsed your material. You know your ideas are sound and you've got a convincing argument that you know will carry the day. So just do it. Commit to what you've prepared. Believe in yourself. Believe in all the hard work you've put into developing your ideas and then figuring out how to present them. You've worked hard to get to this point. Now the idea is to just relax and deliver. And one other thing—have fun.

If you've done everything we've discussed here, and you really know your stuff, you can overcome some pretty daunting obstacles. Even the one Sally Hogshead encountered in this story.

*Sitting in LA morning traffic, I felt like an antelope being digested by a python. Slowly, slowly being constricted through a long tunnel of freeway. I was finally deposited at my client's doorstep, approximately ten seconds before the start of the new business presentation.*

*This was still early in my career, but my partner and I had worked for weeks on the presentation, so I felt confident about the outcome. At least, I felt confident until I reached into the back seat for the portfolio case. . . .*

*Wait. The portfolio case . . . Where's the frikkin' portfolio case?!! As icy water flushed through my blood, I realized exactly where the portfolio case was: on the kitchen counter.*

*Um, yeah.*

*Lesson #1: Don't forget the stuff you're there to present.*

*Most of us spend a lot of time on the material in the presentation, and very little on the presentation itself. But dumping your notes into PowerPoint slides is akin to serving Bobby Flay cuisine on dirty paper plates.*

*For anyone working in an idea-based business, coming up with ideas doesn't mean squat if you can't sell them. We sell ideas in presentations—whether those presentations take place in a boardroom or a coworker's cubicle—which means that presentations form the very building blocks of our careers.*

*In today's marketing environment of chaos and insecurity, you have to fortify your ideas to face the most hairy decision-making moments. Below, a few tips for turning great hypothetical ideas into great produced ideas.*

**Think of the client's concerns before they do.**

*Ahead of the meeting, be brutally honest with yourself and your team in pinpointing the weak spots in your ideas. That way, you can address those if the client brings them up. Consider all the aspects of your client's needs, concerns, insecurities, politics, and biases that you'll have to overcome in order to earn their genuine consideration. The point isn't to defensively fight for your work, but rather, to avoid being caught flat-footed by a tough question.*

**Be able to articulate every element of your recommendations.**

*Don't send your ideas out alone and defenseless into the meeting. Be able to clearly explain every element of your work, why you did things the way you did, and the reasoning behind it. Odds are that you didn't develop your recommendations by randomly shooting darts at a spreadsheet; make sure the client understands why you did what you did.*

**If the presentation starts sucking wind, don't wait to find out what's going wrong.**

*Instead of nervously pushing forward to make it out alive, try to rustle the pink elephant out of the bushes. Acknowledge the situation with a little diplomatic honesty: "I could be wrong, but by those veins throbbing in your temples, I'm sensing that this isn't working for you." Only once they express their concerns can you then redirect attention to solving them.*

**Finally, check the kitchen counter before you walk out the door.**

*(Just to be safe.)*

—Sally Hogshead, speaker, writer, brand consultant, author
of *Fascinate: Your 7 Triggers to Persuasion and Captivation*

Sally forgot her case, but she nailed it anyway, because she was ready.

She knew the material and had worked on the presentation for weeks with her partner.

She stayed committed.

And, oh yeah, she's Sally Hogshead.

# TEN

# PUNCTUATION

I f you were to write someone a letter, you would use punctuation, right?

When we speak, we use punctuation of a different sort. The commas and periods are heard, not read. But that doesn't mean they're not there—they definitely are.

In a presentation, they *have* to be there. It is critical that we punctuate what we are saying in order to maximize the understanding of our words. Furthermore, if we are speaking for any length of time upwards of a few minutes, it is very difficult to hold an audience's attention without practicing precise punctuation of our words. Put another way, I believe that we must have *empathy* for our audience. We must recognize that listening to anyone for more than a few minutes is difficult, and damn near impossible if they don't punctuate effectively. So we've got to help the audience stay with us.

How do we do this? What do we have at our disposal to punctuate our thoughts?

The answer is: a lot. Let's run down the list and explain a bit about how to put some of them to use.

**Pause.** What happens in the room when we pause? The room becomes silent. For most people, this is terrifying. Most of us are afraid of silence, which is why we speak too fast and attempt to fill all of our allotted airtime with sound. This is an amateurish mistake and makes us look nervous and afraid. Not confident and powerful. People usually don't want to work with folks who are nervous and afraid. I see this a lot with young people. Many young people speak way too quickly to begin with, but then they compound the problem by jamming all the words together into a series of run-on sentences that turn into run-on paragraphs until no one has any idea what they're saying. When I call them on this, they almost invariably say, "Well, I wanted to get it over with." There's a great way to approach a presentation, huh? Why not just skip the whole thing in the first place? That would be even easier. This is, of course, so absurd it hardly merits discussion, but I see it all the time all over the country. These folks would be so much better if they would just slow down and pause from time to time. Don't change anything else. Just stop talking for a beat or two. Silence will help you. Silence will make you appear to be confident and in command. So don't be afraid of silence.

Silence is our friend.

By pausing after each important thought or sentence, we are showing that we are confident.

But, the most important fact about the use of silence: people tend to remember the last thing we say before we become quiet. So, make one of your key points, and be quiet. Wait a beat or two, and then go on to your next idea. This is a very important technique to master, because it tells the audience exactly what we want them to think about.

Using silence for punctuation is one of simplest techniques you can use to instantly appear to be a better presenter. More importantly, you actually *will* be a better presenter, because your judicious use of silence is letting the audience know which ideas are the key thoughts.

The key thoughts should be spoken as if they were your headlines. In fact, I try to speak only in headlines. No body copy. Now, I will break that rule time and again when I sense the potential of a digression to help me make my point, but I will quickly return to headlines. Watch a Steve Jobs' MacWorld presentation online. He speaks almost exclusively in headlines. Your use of silence is giving the audience relief from non-stop noise, and is telling them, however subtly, that you are confident in your ideas.

It's one of the key techniques to communicating with Clarity, Conviction, and Grace.

**Volume.** From time to time, change the volume of your voice. You should not stay at the same level throughout your presentation. Punctuate by going up and down in volume. There are times when you will want to shout out a particular thought because it's so important or you're so excited about it, or any number of other reasons. Go ahead and do it. If you don't shout, at least raise your voice a few decibels. At other times, you can use quietness to great advantage. Perhaps to convey a sense of intimacy, or to make a point that is particularly emotional for you. We all remember wonderful storytellers who could virtually whisper key sentences to us and, at other times, would nearly be shouting. Have you ever read a children's book to a kid? Or had one read to you? Remember how the reader changed her volume based on what was happening in the story? It's the same thing with presenting.

Think about a wonderful homily you heard given at church. Or listen to a really skillful politician. They change volume regularly. One tried and true technique is to barrel along picking up momentum and volume. And then deliver what seems to be the key line with the loudest volume you can muster. Followed by the next line, which might truly be the most important, in a very low volume. You see it all the time and it works all the time. You can do the same.

---

### TAKE NOTE

We can all learn from the people around us. Whether it's at a place of worship, a town hall meeting, or on television. Be aware of the techniques that powerful communicators are using to make their points. As we've said elsewhere, do not copy their style.

Your style will be just fine, once you've discovered what's most effective for you. But do pay attention to what great speakers do. There's a lot to be learned.

---

**Pitch.** Staying on one note is monotonous, the root of which is the word "monotone." It means one note. Use as many notes as you can. Think of it as music. I have worked with several folks with musical backgrounds who have found that advice very useful. So play different notes. If you don't, your audience will tire quickly. You don't want that. You want them to be eager to hear more even after you're though. So vary your pitch.

> **IMPORTANT NOTE:**
>
> It is critical that *you* finish before the audience does.

**Tone of voice.** We know how important this is in the overall impression you make on your audience. So don't leave it to chance. Think about it in advance. Decide what tone will work best for each particular section of your presentation. Should you be playful at this point, deadly serious at this, quietly excited here, etc.? What tone is appropriate for that section of your message? In fact, what should your *voice* be for this particular presentation? Years ago, visiting a friend at Leo Burnett, I walked into his office and asked what he was doing. He said that he "was trying to decide what my voice should be for the presentation to Miller Light." He would never change his style, and neither should you, but you should think about the appropriate voice for each situation.

For example, are you going to be the fiery orator, outraged by the wrong done to your client by other agencies? Or the avuncular, quiet voice of a trusted advisor? Maybe you'll be the champion of the people.

You get the idea.

**Facial expressions.** Use your face to advantage. Smile. Smiling works. Not like a model at an automobile show, but when it's appropriate. Change to quizzical when asking a question. Become somber when delivering bad news. Your face is one of the most powerful tools you have.

**Ask questions.** It's a great way to get the audience engaged, which, as we know, is what we want. It breaks up your monologue and creates the illusion of conversation, which is particularly desirable. Get people involved. Get them thinking about the subject matter. Make them a part of the presentation. This will create a more memorable experience for your audience than just sitting there. Because if you let them just sit there, they'll listen for a while and then, eventually, they will drift off to their own thoughts. You know, you've been there.

One technique that I continually use is to start with a question. The very first thing I say, the thing I want to use to get their attention is a question. "Why are we here today?" "Why is it important that we do this?" These kinds of questions get their attention right away and cause them to begin to think, which is good. They usually figure it's a trick question of some kind, so that gets them double-clutching and trying to outguess one another, and me. It's a good way to get things going and to let people know that today's presentation isn't going to be business as usual. And people like that.

**Movement.** Moving with purpose can be a powerful way to punctuate our words. Finish a sentence or phrase in one part of the room, and then become silent while moving to the other side of the room to pick up the next sentence or thought. Many speakers use this technique to great advantage. But many misuse it. Remember the key phrase: "moving with purpose." Just moving will provide relief for the audience, but moving with purpose will underscore your ideas and make it clear to the audience what you want them to retain.

Some wonderful presenters never move, preferring to deliver their thoughts from one powerful position. But these folks are in the minority.

Moving with purpose doesn't have to involve covering a lot of real estate. I frequently have workshop groups tell me how much they appreciated one of their colleagues' use of movement when the person in question might have traveled the width of a conference room table. It's not important that you cover a lot of ground—it's important that you move around.

Moving with purpose communicates a sense of confidence and relaxation on the part of the speaker. It says he's in charge of this space, he's comfortable with it; in fact, it says, not so subtly, this is his space. I've used masculine pronouns in this last sentence because moving around the room seems to be a guy trick. Men are much more likely to move around than women are. I'm not sure why this is, but I've theorized that, just as a dog marks his territory, guys mark their space in rooms. Most women don't. Which is why it is very powerful for a woman to use the technique of moving with purpose. It's seldom done and it really works.

A longtime friend of mine, Nina DiSesa, is a tremendous presenter. One of Nina's techniques, which I've seen her use time and again, is to move around the room, purposefully, with a warm, friendly smile on her face. It's very hard to say no to Nina. Which might have something to do with why she became the first female chairman of McCann Erickson.

**Gestures**. We've got arms and hands, and God knows, we've got to do something with them. Use them to make your intentions clear. Gesture at the appropriate points in your talk. They will serve to provide meaning and relief to the audience. I believe that almost any gestures are helpful until they become distracting. At that point, stop. Watching yourself on video is a good way to see exactly what you might be doing a little too much or too little of with regard to gestures. Failing that, have someone watch and listen to your rehearsal. They can be a big help.

Use your body to communicate. People often ask me about **body language**, and they're right to do so. I'm not a big believer in the "unspoken messages" of body language, but certainly movement, facial expressions, gestures, and just about everything else we do with our bodies is going to help us make a connection. Remember that 55 percent of the information people take away from presentations is Visual?

**Visual aids and props.** Anything on boards, the screen, cards, flip charts, or props of any kind can provide punctuation by attracting the audience's attention for a moment or two. But remember when using any of these devices that *you* are the message. I want you to be the star. Not the screen. (At this point someone may be thinking, "but it's the work that's the star." Not really. Selling the work may in fact be why we're doing the presentation, but in order to buy the work, they're going to have to buy you.)

It is critical that you buy into this simple understanding. **You are the message.** No matter how good the work is, if they don't believe you, if they don't trust you, they won't buy the work. One of the important functions of the presentation format is that it serves as a device to allow people to form an opinion of us, to evaluate us and ultimately decide if they trust us.

Week in and week out, all over the country, I find myself saying, "You are really good. Your slides suck." Over and over, all the time. We've talked about the problems with decks elsewhere, but it can't hurt to repeat it. The slides are meant to be visual aids, not to compete with the presenter for the audience's attention. When we put something up on the screen, what is the audience going to do? They're going to read it. And if you've got a lot of words up there, they're going to try to read them and will ignore you. Even worse, they will read the slides long before you get around to talking about the ideas on the screen. So there is now a huge disconnect in the room and the whole thing has jumped the rails. It happens every day.

It's the same effect as handing out material for people to look at while you speak. They will read the material. They will page ahead. Those interested in what the thing costs will flip ahead to try and find the budget page. They will cease listening to you. So if you want to break off any human connection with your audience, be sure to hand out stuff for them to look at, or project a series of slides with a lot of bullet points and type all over them. They'll tire of you quickly.

**Eye contact.** One of the most powerful techniques we have, both for making an emotional connection with our audience, but also as punctuation, is eye contact. If we are going to connect with our audience, and we had better if we want to persuade them of anything, we need to make eye contact with each person in the room. If there are 5,000 in a ballroom in Vegas, this may be impossible. But you must still look out into the crowd as if you are making eye contact with individuals.

Start each of your sentences by looking directly into someone's eyes.

Switch to someone else when you have finished the thought. Or, you can switch to someone else at the end of a phrase.

Doing this will make an enormous difference in how you are perceived as a presenter. And that's the whole idea, isn't it?

Another important benefit in making legitimate eye contact, eye contact that we use for punctuation, is that it enables us to read the room. Remember, even though you may be doing most of the talking, you need to listen to the people in the room with your ears and your eyes. What you see could make a big difference in the outcome of the presentation. Here's Cindy Gallop talking about something that she saw while presenting to a client.

> *When presenting, it is critically important that you read your audience—via body language, facial expression, mannerisms, etc.—to get a sense of how what you are presenting is being received.*
>
> *If it becomes increasingly clear that something is not being well received, never be afraid to go "off-piste" rather than get through the presentation at all costs.*
>
> *Back in the early days of BBH New York, we were pitching a client, and it became increasingly apparent to me that what we were saying was going down about as well as a cup of cold sick.*
>
> *I stopped the presentation halfway through and said, "Guys—you're clearly not happy with what we're saying. Let's just stop here and talk about it."*
>
> *It transpired that there had been a disconnect in the briefing, and we were way off track in terms of the approach we'd taken. We didn't get the business, but we did at least end the presentation on amicable terms having sorted out what was wrong."*
>
> **—Cindy Gallop, founder, IfWeRanTheWorld,**
> **former chairman, BBH New York**

Here's an example of how simply making effective eye contact can change the way people perceive you. I was working with a group of creative directors one morning in Toronto.

The CEO of the agency sat in just to see what we were up to, since it was my first time at the agency. He had to leave for some meetings midmorning, but he came back in the afternoon when his people were presenting their work. At a break, he took me aside and said, "Wow. Thank you so much. They've improved tremendously. How did you do it?"

All I had done was get the people to practice effective eye contact. They were looking the CEO in the eye when they presented their work. That was the only difference.

It's not necessary to be looking at someone the entire time you're presenting. That could get a little weird. It's fine to look to the heavens for inspiration, or out the window to briefly admire the view. It's natural to look around. But **when you have something important to say, you must be looking at someone.**

We've said repeatedly that presenting effectively is all about making an emotional connection. That emotion is the key to persuasion. Well then, we've got to make effective use of our eyes because, as we've all heard, the eyes are the window to our souls. It's true. People look directly into one another's eyes when they want to connect. Another thing that happens is this—you will see that by making effective eye contact, you are causing your audience to pay closer attention. Because the folks in the audience see that you are making eye contact with their colleagues, they will stare at you, anticipating the moment when you get around to making eye contact with them. And then you've got them.

I keep referring to effective eye contact. What do I mean? Making eye contact for a sufficient length of time. Not too long and not too short. You'll be able to feel it, particularly if you are coordinating what you are saying to the length of your eye contact and are using it for punctuation.

It will feel natural and good to you.

Another important benefit of making effective eye contact is that it says to your audience that you know your stuff and that you're confident.

As we've said elsewhere, people respond to confidence.

You must avoid shifting contact from one person to another quickly. I call this Panning and Scanning and it doesn't say anything except, "I'm nervous and not sure of myself or what I'm saying." Not what we want.

Don't glance at people and then quickly look away and make eye contact with someone else. Subconsciously, what you're doing here is telling the first person that they aren't important and therefore not worthy of your precious attention (eye contact). So once you get on someone, stay on them long enough to make effective contact.

Speaking of the relative importance of people in the room, I'm often asked how to divide your attention among the several people from the client organization. My answer is, spread the love. You may start on the boss, but be sure to give plenty of love to her minions. It's not only the right thing to do, it's the smart thing to do. Unless the boss is a complete megalomaniac, she's watching to see if you respect her people. Which is exactly what her people are doing as well. They want to see if you respect them. If you somehow indicate that you don't—and not looking at them is a pretty clear indicator that you don't—they will make you pay for it later.

The same thing goes for an internal audience. There may be people who are several levels above you in the organization as well as peers and underlings scattered around the room. Share the love.

Speaking of client meetings, what do you and your colleagues do when one of you is presenting? Model the behavior you want the audience to emulate. That means sit there attentively, nodding and smiling while your teammate does his thing. It is great support for your teammate and shows the rest of the audience how to behave. It's important for them to see that you like your teammate and agree with what he's saying. If they don't see that very clearly, they begin to wonder, and a client that begins to wonder is one step closer to saying no.

Using effective eye contact is one of the quickest ways to be seen as a better presenter, but it's important for another very big reason: credibility. It says you're telling the truth. That's why they are looking you in the eye and deciding that you believe what you are saying.

Another benefit of making strong eye contact for some presenters is that it tends to slow them down and focus on each individual in the room. I've seen presenters go from scattered fast talkers to powerful presenters simply by using eye contact.

Invest in a remote that will change the slides on your deck without your having to reach down and push "forward." I know this sounds elementary, but you would be surprised by the number of otherwise credible ad agencies that don't have a remote in their conference rooms. Without a remote, you must look down and push the buttons.

This breaks eye contact with the audience at the two most important parts of your slide—the first sentence and the last. It doesn't really get any better if we have a colleague "drive" the computer for us. So buy a remote. Learn to work with it. Learn to walk around the room and change the slides without looking at the screen. This will make you appear to be a form of wizard to your audience since most presenters spend a good deal of their time checking to see exactly which slide happens to be on the screen at any given time. And then they keep looking back at it even though it hasn't changed and still says exactly what it said the last time they looked at it. This is disconcerting to the audience and makes the presenter look like a nervous person who doesn't know her stuff. It's fine to look at the slide for a moment, but then get back to making effective eye contact with the people in the audience.

Throughout our lives, we've had situations in which people have literally or figuratively asked us to look them in the eye and tell them our story. It's the same thing with presentations.

So look them in the eye and tell them your truth.

Slow down. Take your time. Vary your pitch and volume. Move around the room. Smile where appropriate. Take charge of the room. And get what you came for.

## PRESENTING ON THE PHONE

An unpleasant reality of modern life in advertising is the telephone presentation. Geography, shrinking budgets, and the development of technology are the principal reasons this once-unthinkable practice has proliferated. I say unthinkable, because over the phone is simply not the optimum way of presenting work. We all know this, but telephone presentations aren't going away, so what can we do to optimize our level of success on the phone?

A few thoughts that, not surprisingly, are consistent with many of our recommendations for in-person presentations:

> **Control the visuals.** If you're showing work that is preceded by a deck of some kind, as is so often the case, you've got to have control of that deck. You can't let them flip ahead and read it for themselves. If they can, they will. Which means they won't be paying attention to what you and your colleagues are saying. So use WebEX or any of the other software programs that allow you to control the viewing of the deck. Just as in an in-person presentation, don't let them see any slide until exactly the right moment. Make sure that your slides are in harmony with your words.

**Start Strong.** Get their attention right away. Start with something powerful, urgent, or compelling. Cause them to pay attention throughout the call and understand the importance of doing so.

**Lay Some Ground Rules.** Tell them you know they're busy, just as you are, and if they will cease multitasking during the call, they will actually get a lot more done and get it done more quickly. So ask them to stop emailing or texting.

**Interact Early.** Get folks involved in the call right away by calling them by name. Ask for their input and comments. Solicit the opinions of the quieter people who usually don't speak up. Call on them by name, which emphasizes the need to pay attention.

**Punctuation.** Punctuation is even more important on the phone because unless you're using video conferencing, they can't look at you and respond to you. So use the techniques discussed earlier. Vary your pitch, timbre, speed. Use inflection. Don't be afraid of silence. Although without your body language to follow, you probably can't pause quite as long as you can in person.

**Make It Visual.** They don't have you to look at, so make the deck as visual as possible. Simple, elegant, and restrained use of type. If you're in doubt, err on the side of images rather than type.

You can send them a written document after the call is over. Make this a presentation, not a "group-read" of a PowerPoint deck.

**Stay Committed.** At times there will be silence on the other end. Don't let this throw you. Stay focused and on point. As we said earlier, ask for their reactions if the silence goes on too long. You may consider having a conversation with one of the participants before the presentation and ask them to help out by asking questions and keeping the energy up on their end.

**Don't Try to Do Too Much.** Most phone conferences, like in-person presentations, are too long. Phone fatigue sets in quickly. If you have a lot of material, you may consider not presenting it all on one call. You may schedule another call for another day if possible. Do everything you can to make the call as efficient a use of everyone's time as possible.

**Keep Your People in Line.** Just as we work to command the attention of the folks on the other end of the line, insist that your own people stay engaged and focused. Don't let them email or text during the meeting either, and don't allow them to make faces or gestures at the phone. (We've all seen it. It's stupid and disrespectful.)

**Stand Up.** I believe that standing up is a good idea. It makes it feel more important to the presenters and it lends a different, more powerful tone to your voice. Professional singers don't sit down for a reason. Subconsciously, it communicates a feeling of authority to the listeners.

BBC Radio news presenters were required to wear tuxedos up until World War II. Think about that.

**Plan the Call.** Just as you would a meeting in your board room, plan out the call in advance. Know what you want from it. Be sure that everyone on your team is in complete agreement and understands the strategy for the call. Too many phone conferences are treated like a random chat with a buddy. Make it businesslike and professional.

**Rehearse.** Just as with in-person presentations, rehearsal will make you better. It will help you to be more concise and get to the point quicker. I suggest that you and your team work on phone presentations. Get the team in one room and have the caller call in from another room in your offices. Listen to what it sounds like. Record the calls. Most people who do a lot of telephone presentations have never heard themselves or their teammates this way. When they listen to the playback, they usually discover that they are creating a far different effect than they thought they were. So listen and learn.

If you follow these suggestions and treat the call as a true presentation, with all the planning and creativity that one requires, you'll get more done and you'll sell more of your best work.

Remember, punctuation is even more important on the phone.

## THE ULTIMATE PUNCTUATION MARK: THE CLOSE

We've discussed the importance of a strong opening and a powerful ending. We're telling a story, remember? These are critical components to any presentation and it's useful to think of the opening and the close as punctuation marks.

But how are they delivered, and more to the point, who delivers them?

In the last chapter, Darren Moran mentioned his practice of "casting" the appropriate people both to create the presentation and to deliver it. Remember, they may not be the same people. Different people have different strengths. With that in mind, the best agencies are aware of the talents of each of their people with regard to presenting. They know who can open a meeting with excitement, who can deliver a thoughtful, compelling, and logical setup to the work or ideas, who can really bring the presentation of those ideas to life, and, maybe most importantly, who can close the deal. We've all heard of the concept of the "closer" in business vocabulary, that person who stands up, wraps it all up, and delivers a few well-chosen remarks that make the client say "yes." I've seen many good closers over the years. They come in all different sizes and shapes. But the one thing they all have in common is the ability to excite the imagination of the audience. To challenge them to be their "best selves."

To inspire them to something greater, more significant. To raise the level of discourse. Sometimes it's done with a story, other times with some kind of device or prop. However it's done, more often than not, they get what they came for.

Agencies that win a lot have a closer. Who's yours? If you don't know, find one.

I won't get into naming a list of the best closers I've ever seen, but I will quote my colleague, Don Just, who's been the president of at least two important ad agencies over the years and knows how to close.

*The pitch was to a major American jeans manufacturer—important to the agency as it would be our first well-known, highly visible national consumer brand with a large advertising budget. We went all out to prepare a comprehensive strategic and spec creative presentation that filled our allotted three-hour time slot.*

*We were assigned the first presentation slot among the five finalists, and presentations began on Monday with one per day during the week. The audience consisted of a dozen or so client execs, including marketing, advertising, and management types from around the country. Presentations were held in a very large, empty warehouse-type building; in the middle of the room was a long table behind which were seated the client reps.*

*The presentation proceeded well, moving from in-depth research findings to my specific strategic and tactical recommendations to a lengthy creative pitch. At the end, much of the room was filled with creative materials, from packaging to signage to advertising to fully mocked-up store displays, and, through it all, the clients maintained a stoic demeanor, never indicating approval, excitement, or enthusiasm for any of the work. In fact, toward the end of the pitch, during an animated presentation of TV spots, the lead dog got up and said, "I've seen enough," and left the room—disconcerting, to say the least.*

*Our biggest problem, though, was how to keep our presentation alive and in the minds of the client for the entire week as they moved from presentation to presentation. What we did was simple but proved to be highly effective. The room's ceiling was high, perhaps 20 feet, and there was only one entrance/exit door. Having scouted the room ahead of time, we brought a ladder which I climbed to place a strip of duct tape four or five feet above the door. From the top of the ladder I thanked the client for including us, asked for the business and directed their attention to the tape, saying, "We've put the mark on the wall. Each time you leave a subsequent presentation, look at this mark, and if what you have just seen was better, then replace this mark with theirs. However, if, at the end of the week, our mark is still on the wall, then your decision should be easy."*

*On Friday afternoon of presentation week, I received a call from the client who said, "Your mark is still on the wall. Congratulations, you're our new agency."*

**—Don Just, professor, VCU Brandcenter**

# ELEVEN

# YOU NEVER KNOW

I am the first to admit that that there are an awful lot of things about which I know very little. Or nothing. Many times in the day I find myself saying, "I don't know." (By the way, the next time I hear a politician say that, it will be the first time. Please point out a politician who says, "I don't know, but I've got a lot of smart people who work for me, and they'll find the answer. Then I'll get back to you." I'll vote for him/her.)

But there is one thing I definitely do know, and that is that you never know.

You never know when there is someone in the room who can really help/hurt you. You never know when something you have said or done in the past will come back to reward/haunt you. You cannot take any situation for granted. You've got to be at your very best at all times. Everything is a presentation, remember?

Let me illustrate this point. Years ago, my agency was invited to participate in a presentation for something that seemed like an exciting piece of business. We felt that way until we found out that the invitation wasn't exactly exclusive. There would be 24 other agencies presenting, and we were all going to do it on the same day. That's right, 24 agencies on one day. The plan, if one can call it that, was to give each agency 15 minutes to make its case.

Our first reaction was to say thanks but no thanks. It seemed like a ridiculous proposition, and more to the point, a clear indication of the low regard in which the prospective client held agencies and what they do.

But we thought about it for a while and decided that it really couldn't hurt to participate. Because, you never know.

So I took a day and traveled five hours round trip to make my 15-minute presentation. I thought it went well, but I really didn't expect anything to happen.

And then, something did. The very next day, I got a call from the person in charge of the cattle-call presentation. He said, "We're not going to hire your agency. We're going to hire J. Walter Thompson because they're famous and everyone has heard of them. I was just helping these folks with this review. I'm the director of marketing of Riggs National Bank [an account with a much larger budget]. Would you guys like to talk about being our agency?" I quickly answered, "Yes."

Two weeks later, we had the account. We didn't even have to compete for it. The client was so impressed with the work that we showed in our 15-minute presentation that he wanted to learn more about us. When he did, he decided to hire us, saying, "I really liked a lot of your work, I just didn't know you were the guys who did it."

We worked on that account for years and produced some of the very best, most awarded, most effective work in our agency's history.

You never know.

Another thing I've learned in all the years I've been involved with agencies and clients is that **if you do what the client, or new business prospect expects you to do—they will be disappointed.** You need to go above and beyond and bring them something that surprises and delights them. Here's a story from Jeff Steinhour that brings that idea to life.

*Let's call this "The Element of Surprise."*

*You'll hear all kinds of advice on making presentations and becoming a stand-out presenter from pros that do it for a living. But one thing that many won't mention is digging for the unexpected and delivering something fresh that no one might have seen coming. This only really works once you've surmised the requisite "deliverables" and feel very confident that you have the data you need to carry the day in your meeting. Sometimes showing true skill comes after knowing you've done the expected work and have time to go deeper and further.*

*When we (CP+B) were asked to consider a project for struggling Burger King in 2003, we were caught off guard. BK had six agencies on their roster, and we were asked for some ideas on a particular assignment. The more we thought about how to help them, the more we realized we'd need to get deeper to uncover the real issues, not just ruin a weekend coming up with some TV spots. So we asked about taking a shot at delivering ideas for the whole account—a bit crazy at the time. The CMO was open to it and the more we all thought about it, the more he warmed up to really going for it. So we asked for an extra day, yes, a day to do this. That was really all the time allowed. A weekend plus a day to try and sort out the BK business and brand opportunities. Foolish? Maybe. But about 40 people went off on it for 48 hours straight and uncovered some amazing insights, facts, and issues. It was all organized in a linear way that gave the clients a path toward success that couldn't be skipped or supplanted with short cuts. And when we presented to them, in what they expected would be the result of a weekend spent writing funny scripts and gags, it was something entirely different. In what became a four-hour meeting at our office in Miami, we gave them a solid, wall-to-wall three hours of business observations on their franchise and how it needed to change and evolve. Not one ad or marketing idea was shown for over three straight hours. And they were enthralled. What they saw were ideas for products, their stores, their uniforms, their parking lots, the way traffic flowed through the real estate, signage, the language they used in their stores, the names for their internal materials, the way they hired, where their competitors were weak, how they'd abandoned their "star," the Whopper, and much more. And then finally they saw some ads. In hour four.*

*What they expected was the furthest thing from what they received and it really mattered to show the depth of digging, the passion, the hard news about how some things they were doing really sucked. And they said to us, after four hours of smart business ideas, "How do we get started with you guys?" By executing many of the pitch ideas, beginning in January 2004, together we produced 63 straight months of positive same-store sales, month after month. This had not happened in over a decade for their brand. A long way to say, do not be afraid to share what you think is most important with your allotted time. Almost all discussions around preparing for a big meeting involve answering what the intended audience is expecting to see. Go further, have a sharp point of view, and believe that it needs to be heard. And have the courage to win.*

**—Jeffrey Steinhour, president and managing partner, Crispin Porter + Bogusky Advertising**

Once we were invited on a truly bizarre presentation boondoggle. Our agency was invited to London, along with representatives from 23 other agencies from the United States and Europe, in order to meet with a big international client.

It was, of course, ridiculous. But I went, because you never know.

What ensued was a week-long magical mystery tour through the British Isles visiting the client's manufacturing plants.

I won't go into the hilarious tales that came from that week. I'll just say that at the end of the week, we were invited to spend some time thinking about what we might do to help this client and then send our thoughts, ads, ideas, etc., to them. In a box through the mail. Today, I would never do that. I insist on being in the room to present. But if I had done that then, I would have been wrong. Because we sent in our package of ideas, and made it to the next round of six agencies to present in person in New York City. See, you never know.

We went to New York, and made it to the final round of two agencies to present back in England at an inn outside London.

We turned up there and, I thought, did a great job.

Just not great enough.

Our competitors had included not just spec creative in their offering, but fully produced creative which was ready to run.

They won, and the stuff ran.

We were told that we were wonderful lads and that we'd be hearing from them soon. Yeah, right.

In a few days, we got a letter saying that they really appreciated our efforts and hoped to work with us on something else someday. Yeah, right.

Two months later, I got a phone call from the president of the North American office of this company, awarding us his account, which was considerably more exciting and lucrative than the original one we'd pitched for. As I said, you never know.

Here's a slightly different, but no less important way that "you never know" works.

Once, I was the president of the Richmond Advertising Club. At one of our officers' meetings, a young lady from the Virginia Commonwealth University undergraduate advertising club came to present a report to us on the activities of the students' club. She did a fantastic job and impressed us all very much. Fifteen months later she came to my agency looking for a job. I agreed to see her because I remembered how impressive she had been in her presentation to our group. But I had to tell her that we weren't going to hire any junior account people. She countered by saying she would do anything just to get her foot in the door. I thought about it a minute and then asked her if she'd be willing to take a job as my assistant. She agreed to it on the spot, and she became our newest employee shortly thereafter. She had gotten her foot in the door at the agency she wanted to work for principally because of a presentation she had given to me and a few of my fellow officers 15 months before. So again, you never know.

But there's more to the story. She performed her way out of the job as my assistant pretty quickly and soon became an account executive, and a very good one, indeed. After a few years, she left us for another agency, where she worked for a few years, and then went to the client side, always moving up in title and opportunity.

During all this time, she and I remained friends, and she would regularly call on me for career advice and guidance. I was always happy to offer it.

To make a long story a little bit shorter, today that young lady is in charge of the marketing and advertising for a Fortune 50 company. She still calls on me regularly, but now she is my client and I work for her. We've come full circle.

You never know.

So always remember this—if you are going to present, do the very best job you possibly can. Do not hold anything back. Don't ever go through the motions. There can be only one level of effort and that's pedal to the metal. Because you are being judged on how you perform every time out. You owe it to yourself, your firm, your teammates, and your client to give your very best.

You can learn from every presentation. Each presentation should make you and your agency better, tougher. Each presentation, win or lose, is a renewable resource that should be built upon.

## IT'S ALL ABOUT THE AUDIENCE

So get as good at presenting as you possibly can. And then always remember this—it's not about you, it's about the audience. Great presenters know this. They know their material so well and they have rehearsed how they want to present it so well that all they're thinking about is the audience. They are in such tune with the audience that they can adjust their presentation to what is going on in the room. They don't have to stick to their "rehearsed pitch"; they go where they have to go to get what they want. And that may not be in the script.

And besides, you never know.

One thing I do know, and you can be sure of as well, is that storytelling, which we mentioned in Chapter One, is one of the keys to winning over an audience. Not slides and charts, but facts woven into a powerful, logical story and delivered from the heart. A great story can move a tough audience, even one as tough as the Commissioner of the National Basketball Association.

*My most memorable presentation has to be when I suggested to David Stern what he had to do with the NBA's advertising in 2007. It was memorable because that presentation was an epiphany that has affected my presentations ever since—a breakthrough of understanding that came out of a lot of hard work, hand-wringing, brainstorming, research, meticulous preparation and the fear of presenting to David Stern.*

*David Stern, the commissioner of the National Basketball Association, is a notoriously tough customer. Known for his smarts and shrewd intellect, the man has presided over five league lockouts during his tenure, with another negotiating war looming on the horizon as I write this. His record? 5 wins, 0 losses. Waltzing into NBA headquarters in New York and schmoozing Stern and the NBA with some ad jargon and presentation hijinks wasn't going to happen. He was going to rip the agency a new one if we didn't give the presentation of our lives. Or at least a very good one. In fact, I was working for Goodby, Silverstein & Partners at the time and we even had a history of Stern-shellackings. No less a planning presentation guru than Jon Steel recalled Stern's toughness in his book* Truth Lies and Advertising: The Art of Account Planning. *The best planner in history representing the very same agency had been taken to the woodshed by the Commish. Great. So, walking in, I had that going for me.*

*So what did I do? Anticipating Stern's tough defense took me back to the fundamentals. I went back to the very basics of presenting and focused on preparing and delivering a powerful narrative, a story that would capture the NBA's attention right up front and hook them into hearing the resolution. No trickery. No what if's or assumptions. All hard facts, data and thinking woven into a story that walked Stern through the argument, not unlike a lawyer (which Stern is) presenting a case in court.*

*Was it the greatest presentation of all time? Certainly not. But it worked. I was able to line up a strategy that survived the scrutiny of a tough audience and tee'd up our creative. More importantly, the strategy framed our creative as a solution. Which, in all honesty, it was. To this day, in all my presentations, I try*

*to focus on strong facts and logic and how they can tell a story,*
*always looking for holes or weak points.*
*And I've thanked David Stern several times for that.*

**—Andy Grayson, group strategy director,**
**Wieden + Kennedy**

I love Andy's tale because it's about storytelling but also because he refers to so much of what we've been discussing in this book—the importance of hard work, questioning ourselves, excluding the extraneous, meticulous preparation, grabbing the audience's attention right from the start, and having the courage to stand up and express our point of view.

# AFTERWORD

## STANDING UP

Early in my career I learned the value of being a powerful presenter. Even as an agency principal with a hundred different tasks on my plate, I made it a priority to study and learn about presenting in all its forms. I knew that it was important enough to be the difference between success and failure for my firm. But I also knew that it was critical to my personal success and growth. I learned that presenting was a powerful way of expressing not just what I believed, but *who I am*. The way in which we behave in front of an audience while communicating whatever it is that's on our minds says volumes about who we are. If a client is to trust us, she must believe us. And we prove ourselves worthy of that trust by standing up and speaking our truth. If we expect people to follow us, we must inspire them to do so. We must stand up and *be* a leader. On a more mundane level, if we expect someone to buy our work, to embrace our ideas, we must first stand up and convince them that we are worthy of their confidence.

Standing up for our ideas, our work, indeed *ourselves,* isn't easy. We're open to the scrutiny of everyone in the room, virtually naked in the face of their criticism. In order to do it, to get up and win them over, we've got to first believe in ourselves. We've got to believe that what we have to offer will be a significant contribution. In fact, we've got to begin to think of *ourselves* as a contribution. This way of thinking requires an audacity of spirit, a conviction that what we have to share will enrich the conversation and that yes, ultimately, everything will work out for the best. Simply put, it requires courage. It isn't enough to master the techniques and concepts discussed in this book and all the other information sources available to us. Knowledge alone is not the answer. Putting that knowledge to work is the task. This is an exercise in results, not intentions. Accomplishing change, transforming the beliefs of the people in the room, is the achievement.

Defy the conventional, create the exceptional. That's what I'm preaching. Create exceptional work. Create exceptional presentations. Create an exceptional life. Doing so requires standing up.

Most of us are not willing to risk what we think it takes to harness this personal power and transform our lives. But it's not because we're afraid to fail. It's because we're afraid that we'll succeed. That is what truly terrifies us.

When I first read them, I knew immediately that Marianne Williamson's words in *A Return to Love* were a perfect message to share with my students. By the conclusion of a workshop, the students will have spent two days working hard, learning, sharing, and grappling with their own assessments of themselves. They will have confronted the realization that they have the ability to become powerful presenters. The big question is whether they will have the courage to see themselves for who they are and what they can be, or if they will choose to settle for something less than their best selves.

Many people choose to settle. It's too scary to be really good. It causes one to stand out from the crowd, and most people really just want to blend in.

Marianne Williamson says this:

Our deepest fear is not that we are inadequate. Our deepest fear is that we are powerful beyond measure. It is our light, not our darkness, that most frightens us. We ask ourselves, who am I to be brilliant, gorgeous, handsome, talented and fabulous? Actually, who are you not to be? You are a child of God. Your playing small does not serve the world. There is nothing enlightened about shrinking so that other people won't feel insecure around you. We are all meant to shine, as children do. We were born to make manifest the glory of God within us. It is not just in some; it is in everyone. And, as we let our own light shine, we consciously give other people permission to do the same. As we are liberated from our fear, our presence automatically liberates others.[1]

We've discussed the fear that most people have of public speaking or presenting, but the fear that Williamson refers to is far more insidious. It's the fear that keeps us from being who we're capable of being. It's the fear behind low self-esteem. It's the fear that locks us into a life of mediocrity. We have a vision of what our "perfect life" could be, but we don't want to be "that person."

We don't want to stand out when it's oh so much easier to just be one of the crowd. We'd rather "play small." We don't want to jeopardize our personal relationships by becoming "too big." We want everyone to like us, and by living up to our true potential, we run the risk of "showing off," of separating ourselves from the herd. Of being *different*.

I've spent many years trying to help people be different. My purpose has become helping people and organizations realize their fullest potential through the power of communication. Reaching that potential requires that we be *perceived* as different, and in order to achieve that we must actually *be* different.

This difference manifests itself in being perceived as smarter, more creative, funnier, stronger, brighter, cooler, *better* than other people or organizations.

People like Alex Bogusky, Jon Steele, John Adams, Jeff Steinhour, Jamie Barrett, Marshall Ross, and agencies like Crispin Porter + Bogusky, Goodby, Silverstein and Partners, Boone Oakley, The Martin Agency, Mother, and Wieden + Kennedy among many others.

People in our industry admire these individuals and agencies precisely because they are different. They think and act differently from their competitors and from most of the rest of us.

That's because they're not afraid to dream big, defy convention, and fight for the exceptional.

They're not afraid to stand up.

# ACKNOWLEDGMENTS

A few years ago, I was in Japan with my late friend and colleague Andrew Jaffe. We were there as part of a contingent from the VCU Brandcenter, engaged by Dentsu, the globe-spanning advertising firm. Our mission was to teach our Western ways to Dentsu executives from every department in the agency. Presentation was a significant part of the curriculum, and indeed, the way in which the students made manifest their answers to the problems and cases we assigned them.

Andrew had been the driving force behind the Sohatsu Labo, as the training program came to be known. We had known one another for many years, first when Andrew was an editor with *Adweek* magazine and, later, the head of the Clios.

It was during our time in Japan that Andrew urged me to write a book about presenting. He brought it up regularly, both there and once we'd returned to the States. He came to my home in Richmond, Virginia, to talk about his ambitions for the book and to offer encouragement. I wrote a first draft. Andrew said he liked it, but suggested that I start over and get more of my stories and myself into it.

As I was in the process of doing just that, Andrew passed away after a long struggle with cancer.

It was at this point that I committed to seeing this project through. Without Andrew and his encouragement, there would be no book. Thank you, Andrew.

As with just about everything in my life, my wife, Cynthia, has been a rock of support and a wise counselor. She has put up with more from me in the years of our marriage than most people ever would. And then she endured my writing this book.

Thanks to everyone who contributed their personal stories and anecdotes to the book. You're not just spectacularly accomplished, you're kind and generous. You've given it an array of flavors I never could have conjured on my own.

All the students I've taught at the VCU Brandcenter have made valuable contributions as well, as have the participants in my many workshops over the years. I hope I've taught half as much as I've learned. And thanks to all my colleagues on the faculty. A special shout-out to Avery Oldfield and Megan Powers for their help with chapter seven and Marc Andrew Stephens for his photos.

My sons, Peter and Ryan, had nothing to do with the writing of this book, but this seems like an opportunity to put my pride in them into print.

And finally, thanks to my editor, Laurie Harting, her assistant, Tiffany Hufford, as well as Alan Bradshaw, at Palgrave Macmillan. You've made this a better book than it would have been if I had been left to my own devices.

# NOTES

CHAPTER 1

1. *New Oxford American Dictionary* (online edition).
2. Garr Reynolds, *Presentation Zen* (blog), January 24, 2008, http://www .presentationzen.com/presentationzen/2008/01/

CHAPTER 2

1. Lau Tzu, *Tao Te Ching,* translation by Gia-fu Feng and Jane English (London: Wildwood House, 1991; first published 1972).

CHAPTER 3

1. Mehrabian's findings were published in two documents: Albert Mehrabian and Morton Wiener, "Decoding of Inconsistent Communications," *Journal of Personality and Social Psychology* 6, no. 1 (May, 1967): 109–114; and Albert Mehrabian and Susan R. Ferris, "Inference of Attitudes from Nonverbal Communication in Two Channels," *Journal of Consulting Psychology* 31, no. 6 (June, 1967): 248–252.
2. D. Joel Whalen, *I See What You Mean: Persuasive Business Communication* (Thousand Oaks, CA: Sage Publications, Inc., 1995).

CHAPTER 6

1. Agnes de Mille, *Martha: The Life and Work of Martha Graham* (New York: Random House, 1991), p. 264.
2. James C. Collins, Jerry I. Porras, *Built to Last: Successful Habits of Visionary Companies* (New York: Harperbusiness, 1997).

3. Ibid., p. 224.
4. Roy M. Spence Jr., *It's Not What You Sell, It's What You Stand For: Why Every Extraordinary Business Is Driven by Purpose* (New York: Portfolio, 2009).

CHAPTER 7

1. Anna Patty, "Research Points the Finger at PowerPoint," *The Sydney Morning Herald,* April 4, 2007, http://www.smh.com.au/articles/2007/04/03/1175366240499.html.

CHAPTER 9

1. Carmine Gallo, *The Presentation Secrets of Steve Jobs: How to Be Insanely Great in Front of Any Audience* (New York: McGraw-Hill, 2009).

AFTERWORD

1. Marianne Williamson, *A Return to Love: Reflections on the Principles of a Course in Miracles* (New York: HarperCollins, 1992). From chapter 7, section 3 (pp. 190–191).

# INDEX